Love Stories

From the Bible

The Rev George Young, The Rev Anne Bridgers, The Registers (all of them), my sisters, my brother–in-law Hal Thomas, my parents, and my mentor, Mary May. Finally, there are the individuals who have recently said, "Write on"——Bev Browning, Gay Norton Edelman, Rhett and Robert, their beautiful wives, and my beloved Robert Otis Freeman.

My heartfelt thanks to all of you.

Thanks be to God,

Victoria

Acknowledgments

Lots of folks helped me write this book. My third grade teacher Mrs. Wooten saw me as someone who could tell a good story. My fifth grade teacher, Florence Revere, elevated storytelling to new heights. Professor Gabriele Rico helped me commit my stories to print. Greg Krech and Dr. David Reynolds taught me to resist the paralysis of analysis and bring my stories to life.

Then there were those other folks who have walked with me down the life path, feeding me spiritually, physically and mentally: The Rev. Frank Prince,

Dedication

For Nell "Mimi" Hutchins, my grandmother, who listened to my stories with rapt attention and who walked with me to the library every Thursday.

Love Stories From the Bible
Twenty-one Couples Who Still Have a Thing or Two to Teach Us About Romance and Life

by Victoria Register-Freeman

Unless otherwise identified, all Scriptural quotations are taken from the New International Version of the Bible. Copyright ©1973, 1978, 1984 by the International Bible Society. Used by permission of Zondervan Bible Publishers.

Library of Congress Catalog Card Number: Pending
International Standard Book Number: 088270964X

Published by:
Bridge-Logos
Gainesville, FL 32614
bridgelogos.com

Love Stories From the Bible

VICTORIA REGISTER-FREEMAN

Bridge-Logos

Gainesville, Florida 32614 USA

Introduction

One could say that I was born for romance. I came by it rightly. I grew up in the tiny town of Jonesboro, Georgia, the mythic home of Tara, the home place of Scarlett O'Hara and Rhett Butler. By the time I reached adolescence (and full-fledged Southern Belle-hood), I was hopelessly in love with love. But as all young Belles who grew up in the 1950s will attest, romance would have to wait until the time was fitting and proper. Until that time, church was what one did: all day Sunday, Wednesday night and two weeks during summer vacation. In a pre-pill time before cable television, DVD, Walkman and Internet hookup, the Good Book served as my major source of entertainment and illumination. My friends and I were as familiar with the racy exploits of Rahab-the-Harlot as today's teens are with the nocturnal shenanigans of Britney Spears.

During the era before air conditioning, the Bible stories gave us something to do on steamy summer evenings besides begging rides to the Tastee Freeze. Via our imaginations we were Hagar sobbing over Abraham's cowardly choices, Jezebel plotting to get the vegetable patch for her husband, or Mrs. Pilate sending the desperate note to her husband. Martha Carol, the first one of us to develop breasts, always got to play Bathsheba and to come timidly before the king wearing her mom's blue chenille bathrobe. Once in awhile the old boxer dog Deanie would be pulled into action as Abraham's sacrificial ram.

In addition to providing plots for our dramas, the Bible stories also formed us. They gave us our mores and our metaphors. When someone was called a Zipporah, we all knew her personality would be biting. Jezebels were not to be trusted. A Martha was a good person to have around if one wanted somebody to help clean up after the slumber party.

Three decades and many miles from Jonesboro, I find that the Bible is more than my personal love letter from God. It forms the headwaters for the great metaphor river that flows through our English language. Allen Hirsh in the book *Cultural Literacy* states that much of our modern metaphor—the shorthand of the educated class—is Bible-based (while another high percentage comes from William Shakespeare, who lifted a lot of his best phrases from the Bible). Knowing Bible characters and key events helps an individual to decode many a modern message, as well as to deepen one's personal understanding of God's plan.

Therefore, this slender volume is my attempt to introduce (or reintroduce) some biblical characters to you in an appealing context, the context of relationship. You'll find biblical text for each couple following each couple's love lesson if you want to read further. We are becoming a high tech society that craves high touch—contact with other human beings. Knowing the biblical stories of relationship helps us both form and reform our relationships. After all, as my football lovin' papa said on more than one occasion, "Real life, honey, is a contact sport."

Victoria Register-Freeman

Love Stories From the Bible

Adam & Eve

GOD GIVES ABUNDANT GRACE

ADAM & EVE

Talk about stress—Adam and Eve were the point people for the entire human platoon. She was the first woman, the first wife, the first mom and the first grandma. In the Pre-Raphaelite paintings, she always looks like a cross between Goldie Hawn and Malibu Barbie. He was evidently something of a dilettante: naming the animals, picking the sacred fruit, looking for a mate, talking with the Deity.

Their existence seemed blissful at first, a Club Med life where everything was included. They did not have to work. Their sole responsibility was to simply wander around the plantation and avoid a certain large tree in the back forty that their landlord had said was off limits. Perhaps it was that restriction that got to her—like Scarlett who wanted Ashley because she couldn't have him. After awhile the tree began to look interesting. Enter the serpent that played to her desire for novelty and power. *A bite of the fruit and VOILA*, said the snake. *One would always get the best seat at the barbecue.* So Eve bit and reality hit.

Love Lesson 1 **Today, Eve would certainly be a candidate for counseling by Oprah's beloved Dr. Phil. "What were you thinking, Miss Eve?" he would say, hands clasped behind him, warm beagle eyes staring straight at her, "Sounds to me like you shimmied up the dumb tree and hit every branch falling down."**

Nevertheless, there is something reassuring about Eve's adventure. My friend Yasmine, who works weekends in Ezell's BBQ and Dinner

Theater, points out that Eve is a classic example of God-given resilience. "Sure," says Yasmine knowingly "She led Adam into sin—serious sin, but after trying to pass the responsibility buck to the snake, she accepted the consequences of her action. She downsized and dealt with some of the most serious disappointments a woman can have—loss of home, death of a child, disappearance of leisure and there is no mention of her whining. She just did what needed to be done. I know lots of women who make a serious mistake and then spend the rest of their lives with runny noses in support groups rehashing their errors. Eve didn't do that.

"She and Adam got kicked out of the original gated community, and they survived. Even though she must have been disappointed because Adam was so quick to blow the whistle on her during the serpent episode, they obviously remained lovers. After all, there was Seth, the child she had after Abel was killed by Cain. She was definitely a trooper."

My friend Allison, a teacher of religion, notes that Eve did perform a service for mankind. It was through Eve that grace entered into the world. And grace, God's undeserved acceptance and love, has been a lifesaving gift for God's people—saints and sinners—throughout the ages.

Adam & Eve in Scripture

Genesis 3:1-24

[1] Now the serpent was more crafty than any of the wild animals the LORD God had made. He said to the woman, "Did God really say, 'You must not eat from any tree in the garden'?"

[2] The woman said to the serpent, "We may eat fruit from the trees in the garden, [3]but God did say, 'You must not eat fruit from the tree that is in the middle of the garden, and you must not touch it, or you will die.'"

[4] "You will not surely die," the serpent said to the woman. [5] "For God knows that when you eat of it your eyes will be opened, and you will be like God, knowing good and evil."

[6] When the woman saw that the fruit of the tree was good for food and pleasing to the eye, and also desirable for gaining wisdom, she took some and ate it. She also gave some to her husband, who was with her, and he ate it.

[7] Then the eyes of both of them were opened, and they realized they were naked; so they sewed fig leaves together and made coverings for themselves.

[8] Then the man and his wife heard the sound of the LORD God as he was walking in the garden in the cool of the day, and they hid from the LORD God among the trees of the garden.

[9] But the LORD God called to the man, "Where are you?"

[10] He answered, "I heard you in the garden, and I was afraid because I was naked; so I hid."

[11] And he said, "Who told you that you were naked? Have you eaten from the tree that I commanded you not to eat from?"

[12] The man said, "The woman you put here with me — she gave me some fruit from the tree, and I ate it."

13 Then the LORD God said to the woman, "What is this you have done?" The woman said, "The serpent deceived me, and I ate."

14 So the LORD God said to the serpent, "Because you have done this, Cursed are you above all the livestock and all the wild animals! You will crawl on your belly and you will eat dust all the days of your life. 15 And I will put enmity between you and the woman, and between your offspring and hers; he will crush your head, and you will strike his heel."

16 To the woman he said, "I will greatly increase your pains in childbearing; with pain you will give birth to children. Your desire will be for your husband, and he will rule over you."

17 To Adam he said, "Because you listened to your wife and ate from the tree about which I commanded you, 'You must not eat of it,'

"Cursed is the ground because of you; through painful toil you will eat of it all the days of your life. 18 It will produce thorns and thistles for you, and you will eat the plants of the field. 19 By the sweat of your brow you will eat your food until you return to the ground, since from it you were taken; for dust you are and to dust you will return."

20 Adam named his wife Eve, because she would become the mother of all the living. 21 The LORD God made garments of skin for Adam and his wife and clothed them.

22 And the LORD God said, "The man has now become like one of us, knowing good and evil. He must not be allowed to reach out his hand and take also from the tree of life and eat, and live forever."

23 So the LORD God banished him from the Garden of Eden to work the ground from which he had been taken.

24 After he drove the man out, he placed on the east side of the Garden of Eden cherubim and a flaming sword flashing back and forth to guard the way to the tree of life.

Love Stories From the Bible

Abraham & Sarah

ABRAHAM & SARAH:
GOD HONORS COMMITMENT.

ABRAHAM & SARAH

Abraham and Sarah were mostly known for the miracle of their late-in-life infant – "a wee autumn crocus," as my Aunt Maude was fond of saying. Barren for decades of marriage, Sarah conceived Isaac, the son Abraham later agreed to sacrifice as proof of total obedience to God. Those dramatic events—plus the fact that Sarah laughed when God promised pregnancy in spite of her advanced age—gave this couple the distinction of becoming the first pair of lovers that seemed real to me. Sarah herself was especially fascinating. I liked that God changed her name from Sarah to Sarai, meaning "the princess." What Southern Belle couldn't resist the bestowal of a royal title? Sarah followed her husband to Canaan and Egypt. And Sarah, like Scarlett O'Hara, was so gorgeous that even the Pharaoh invited her to party at his palace.

This duo was durable. As Edith Deen, author of several classic Christian conference books, says, "Departure from their native land, the only land either of them had ever known, did not divide them in love or purpose. Sarah never looked back. She shared her husband's dangers and heartaches and also his great purpose and dreams."

Love Lesson 2 **As an adult now, I find Sarah and Abraham helpful in our zip code-hopping world. According to the Bible, Sarah and her husband were in their sixties and seventies when they began their wanderings. Many of my friends have had to conquer the extreme** discomfort that comes along with mid-life relocations, when love for the husband supersedes love for the community.

Pauline, my workout buddy, took comfort from Sarah's story when her husband, a CPA, asked her to consider a move from the Sunshine State to Wisconsin at a time in life when most people from the north (and in their right minds) are considering a move to Florida. "All I knew about Wisconsin," said Pauline, "was that its license tag said something like Eat Cheese." Still, Mark really wanted to go, so I agreed. We're stronger as a couple now because we're strangers in a strange land. The first year was tough, but now we've settled into a good church family. We've even bought two cheese hats to wear to the Packers football games."

She shared her husband's dangers and heartaches and also his great purpose and dreams.

The other lesson from Sarah and Abraham is that children born late in life are blessings from God—even if 90-year-old Sarah and 100-year-old Abraham did fall down laughing when God announced that they were about to be new parents.

Abraham & Sarah in Scripture
Genesis 17:1-27, 18:1-15

[1]When Abram was ninety-nine years old, the LORD appeared to him and said, "I am God Almighty; walk before me and be blameless. [2]I will confirm my covenant between me and you and will greatly increase your numbers."

[3]Abram fell facedown, and God said to him, [4]"As for me, this is my covenant with you: You will be the father of many nations. [5]No longer will you be called Abram; your name will be Abraham, for I have made you a father of many nations. [6]I will make you very fruitful; I will make nations of you, and kings will come from you. [7]I will establish my covenant as an everlasting covenant between me and you and your descendants after you for the generations to come, to be your God and the God of your descendants after you. [8]The whole land of Canaan, where you are now an alien, I will give as an everlasting possession to you and your descendants after you; and I will be their God."

[9]Then God said to Abraham, "As for you, you must keep my covenant, you and your descendants after you for the generations to come. [10]This is my covenant with you and your descendants after you, the covenant you are to keep: Every male among you shall be circumcised.

[11]You are to undergo circumcision, and it will be the sign of the covenant between me and you.

[12]For the generations to come every male among you who is eight days old must be circumcised, including those born in your household or bought with money from a foreigner — those who are not your offspring. [13]Whether born in your household or bought with your money, they must be circumcised. My covenant in your flesh is to be an everlasting covenant. [14]Any uncircumcised male, who has not been circumcised in the flesh, will be cut off from his people;

he has broken my covenant."

[15]God also said to Abraham, "As for Sarai your wife, you are no longer to call her Sarai; her name will be Sarah. [16]I will bless her and will surely give you a son by her. I will bless her so that she will be the mother of nations; kings of peoples will come from her."

[17]Abraham fell facedown; he laughed and said to himself, "Will a son be born to a man a hundred years old? Will Sarah bear a child at the age of ninety?" [18]And Abraham said to God, "If only Ishmael might live under your blessing!"

[19]Then God said, "Yes, but your wife Sarah will bear you a son, and you will call him Isaac. I will establish my covenant with him as an everlasting covenant for his descendants after him. [20]And as for Ishmael, I have heard you: I will surely bless him; I will make him fruitful and will greatly increase his numbers. He will be the father of twelve rulers, and I will make him into a great nation. [21]But my covenant I will establish with Isaac, whom Sarah will bear to you by this time next year." [22]When he had finished speaking with Abraham, God went up from him.

[23]On that very day Abraham took his son Ishmael and all those born in his household or bought with his money, every male in his household, and circumcised them, as God told him. [24]Abraham was ninety-nine years old when he was circumcised, [25]and his son Ishmael was thirteen; [26]Abraham and his son Ishmael were both circumcised on that same day. [27]And every male in Abraham's household, including those born in his household or bought from a foreigner, was circumcised with him.

Genesis 18:1–15

[1]The LORD appeared to Abraham near the great trees of Mamre while he was sitting at the entrance to his tent in the heat of the day. [2]Abraham looked up and

saw three men standing nearby. When he saw them, he hurried from the entrance of his tent to meet them and bowed low to the ground.

³He said, "If I have found favor in your eyes, my lord, do not pass your servant by. ⁴Let a little water be brought, and then you may all wash your feet and rest under this tree. ⁵Let me get you something to eat, so you can be refreshed and then go on your way — now that you have come to your servant."

"Very well," they answered, "do as you say."

⁶So Abraham hurried into the tent to Sarah. "Quick," he said, "get three seahs of fine flour and knead it and bake some bread."

⁷Then he ran to the herd and selected a choice, tender calf and gave it to a servant, who hurried to prepare it. ⁸He then brought some curds and milk and the calf that had been prepared, and set these before them. While they ate, he stood near them under a tree.

⁹"Where is your wife Sarah?" they asked him.

"There, in the tent," he said.

¹⁰Then the LORD said, "I will surely return to you about this time next year, and Sarah your wife will have a son."

Now Sarah was listening at the entrance to the tent, which was behind him. ¹¹Abraham and Sarah were already old and well advanced in years, and Sarah was past the age of childbearing. ¹²So Sarah laughed to herself as she thought, "After I am worn out and my master is old, will I now have this pleasure?"

¹³Then the LORD said to Abraham, "Why did Sarah laugh and say, 'Will I really have a child, now that I am old?' ¹⁴Is anything too hard for the LORD? I will return to you at the appointed time next year and Sarah will have a son."

¹⁵Sarah was afraid, so she lied and said, "I did not laugh."

But he said, "Yes, you did laugh."

Love Stories From the Bible

Lot & Mrs. Lot

LOT & MRS. LOT:
WHEN GOD CALLS YOU FORWARD,
YOU DON'T LOOK BACK.

LOT & MRS. LOT

Mrs. Lot was a country girl who moved into town. The first mention of her was in Genesis 19:15 when the angels came to tell her family to leave Sodom before it was destroyed. Readers are not given any of her characteristics. All we have is her action and God's reaction. *"But Lot's wife looked back and she became a pillar of salt"* (Genesis 19:26).

Before her saline makeover, Mrs. Lot had been the wife of a powerful man. Indeed, the Lots were a couple one might find mentioned in the society column after the ancient equivalent of a gallery opening. As Herbert Lockyear, author of *The Women of the Bible*, says, "Lot became a citizen of Sodom, sat at its gate as the city's mayor, and was treated with honor and reverence as a relative of the mighty Abraham who had delivered Sodom from the Elamite invasion."

Mrs. Lot was a hostess. According to Scripture, she entertained the angels that God had sent to warn the righteous that Sodom was going to be ground zero for God's wrath. After the dinner the angelic deliverers had their hands full when they tried to remove Mrs. Lot from Sodom. She and the entire family were so loathe to leave that the angels had to yell, "HURRY!" Then they followed up with more specific instructions. *"Flee for your lives! Don't look back and don't stop anywhere on the plain!"* (Genesis 19:20).

Mrs. Lot had two daughters. She had doubtlessly heard her husband tell the men who came to molest the guests that they could have the daughters instead. That statement said a great deal about the position of women in Sodom's society. Nevertheless, Sodom was all she knew, and she regretted leaving its glamour. As the wife of a power-figure, she commanded some reflected power herself.

Love Lesson 3   **Myra, the wife of a corporate vice president, sees some parallels in Mrs. Lot's story and her own. She lived an exciting life. Indeed, her life as a corporate vice-president's wife was full of volunteer work, tennis tournaments, and private school PTA. It was, therefore, a shock to her when her husband announced that he felt a growing call to ministry in the Episcopal Church. While she supported his mid-life change through the discernment process, she found herself increasingly conflicted about the loss of her lifestyle.**

"When I saw the tiny house we were going to move into at Sewanee, I cried," confessed Myra. "We had just built our dream house overlooking the Intracoastal Waterway. I didn't think it was right to go through the pain of building and then never live in the house." But the story has a happier ending than Mrs. Lot's salty saga. Entering her second year as a student wife, Myra gives the glory for her change of heart to God, "I asked Him to grant me peace with the process and that is the miracle that happened. Charlie is in his second year in seminary. I have a close group of prayer partners. Life is good. And I don't look back."

Lot & Mrs. Lot in Scripture

Genesis 19:1-36

[1]The two angels arrived at Sodom in the evening, and Lot was sitting in the gateway of the city. When he saw them, he got up to meet them and bowed down with his face to the ground. [2]"My lords," he said, "please turn aside to your servant's house. You can wash your feet and spend the night and then go on your way early in the morning."

"No," they answered, "we will spend the night in the square."

[3]But he insisted so strongly that they did go with him and entered his house. He prepared a meal for them, baking bread without yeast, and they ate. [4]Before they had gone to bed, all the men from every part of the city of Sodom — both young and old — surrounded the house. [5]They called to Lot, "Where are the men who came to you tonight? Bring them out to us so that we can have sex with them."

[6]Lot went outside to meet them and shut the door behind him [7]and said, "No, my friends. Don't do this wicked thing. [8]Look, I have two daughters who have never slept with a man. Let me bring them out to you, and you can do what you like with them. But don't do anything to these men, for they have come under the protection of my roof."

[9]"Get out of our way," they replied. And they said, "This fellow came here as an alien, and now he wants to play the judge! We'll treat you worse than them." They kept bringing pressure on Lot and moved forward to break down the door.

[10]But the men inside reached out and pulled Lot back into the house and shut the door. [11]Then they struck the men who were at the door of the house, young and old, with blindness so that they could not find the door.

[12]The two men said to Lot, "Do you have anyone else here — sons-in-law, sons or daughters, or anyone else in the city who belongs to you? Get them out of

here, [13]because we are going to destroy this place. The outcry to the LORD against its people is so great that he has sent us to destroy it."

[14]So Lot went out and spoke to his sons-in-law, who were pledged to marry his daughters. He said, "Hurry and get out of this place, because the LORD is about to destroy the city!" But his sons-in-law thought he was joking.

[15]With the coming of dawn, the angels urged Lot, saying, "Hurry! Take your wife and your two daughters who are here, or you will be swept away when the city is punished."

[16]When he hesitated, the men grasped his hand and the hands of his wife and of his two daughters and led them safely out of the city, for the LORD was merciful to them. [17]As soon as they had brought them out, one of them said, "Flee for your lives! Don't look back, and don't stop anywhere in the plain! Flee to the mountains or you will be swept away!"

[18]But Lot said to them, "No, my lords, please! [19]Your servant has found favor in your eyes, and you have shown great kindness to me in sparing my life. But I can't flee to the mountains; this disaster will overtake me, and I'll die. [20]Look, here is a town near enough to run to, and it is small. Let me flee to it — it is very small, isn't it? Then my life will be spared."

[21]He said to him, "Very well, I will grant this request too; I will not overthrow the town you speak of. [22]But flee there quickly, because I cannot do anything until you reach it." (That is why the town was called Zoar.)

[23]By the time Lot reached Zoar, the sun had risen over the land. [24]Then the LORD rained down burning sulfur on Sodom and Gomorrah — from the LORD out of the heavens. [25]Thus he overthrew those cities and the entire plain, including all those living in the cities — and also the vegetation in the land. [26]But Lot's wife looked back, and she became a pillar of salt.

[27]Early the next morning Abraham got up and returned to the place where he had stood before the LORD. [28]He looked down toward Sodom and Gomorrah,

toward all the land of the plain, and he saw dense smoke rising from the land, like smoke from a furnace.

²⁹So when God destroyed the cities of the plain, he remembered Abraham, and he brought Lot out of the catastrophe that overthrew the cities where Lot had lived.

³⁰Lot and his two daughters left Zoar and settled in the mountains, for he was afraid to stay in Zoar. He and his two daughters lived in a cave. ³¹One day the older daughter said to the younger, "Our father is old, and there is no man around here to lie with us, as is the custom all over the earth. ³²Let's get our father to drink wine and then lie with him and preserve our family line through our father."

³³That night they got their father to drink wine, and the older daughter went in and lay with him. He was not aware of it when she lay down or when she got up.

³⁴The next day the older daughter said to the younger, "Last night I lay with my father. Let's get him to drink wine again tonight, and you go in and lie with him so we can preserve our family line through our father." ³⁵So they got their father to drink wine that night also, and the younger daughter went and lay with him. Again he was not aware of it when she lay down or when she got up.

³⁶So both of Lot's daughters became pregnant by their father. ³⁷The older daughter had a son, and she named him Moab; he is the father of the Moabites of today. ³⁸The younger daughter also had a son, and she named him Ben-Ammi; he is the father of the Ammonites of today.

Love Stories From the Bible

Abraham & Hagar

ABRAHAM & HAGAR:
GOD WILL PROVIDE FOR US
IN OUR TIME OF GREATEST NEED.

ABRAHAM & HAGAR

The story of Abraham and Hagar reads like many a bodice-ripper paperback. The man wanders over to the trailer park and beds one of its inhabitants, alliteratively known as trailer trash. The wild oats bear a harvest. Problems ensue between the women. The difference in the Hagar story is that Sarah, the lady of the house, sends her husband Abraham to bed Hagar, the other woman, because in the culture of that time offspring born of one's servants could be considered almost one's own (Genesis16: 2-4). Unfortunately, according to Sarah, Hagar begins to strut once she has conceived by Abraham. Sarah is miffed, so miffed that she sends Hagar away into the desert. In Genesis 16: 9 the angel of the Lord finds Hagar and tells her to return to Sarah. The angel sweetens the deal a little by telling Hagar that she will bear a son who will be a handful, but who will link her to "descendants too numerous to count."

As the reader finds out in Genesis 16:15, Hagar bore Abraham a son, and he gave the name Ishmael to the son she had borne. Then the plot thickens. Sarah, who is postmenopausal at age 90, gives birth to her own son Isaac. Now Hagar's son poses a visible threat to the inheritance of Sarah's child. Sarah can't handle the sight of her son playing with Ishmael, so she turns to Abraham and asks him to fix the situation. Genesis 21:11 tells it all *"The matter distressed Abraham greatly because it concerned his son. But God said to him, 'Do not be so distressed about the boy and your maidservant. Listen to whatever Sarah tells you, because it is through Isaac that your offspring will be reckoned. I will make the son of the maid servant into a nation also, because he is your offspring.'"*

Hagar and her son headed for the hills. Soon the water was gone, and that meant death in the desert. Hagar put her son beneath a bush so she would be spared her child's death throes. God intervened. In Genesis 21:17-18 he said, *"Do not be afraid. Lift the boy up and take him by the hand for I will make him a great nation."*

Love Lesson 4   **Hagar is the patron saint of several of my women friends who have been through bad divorces. As Shirley, my favorite beautician/social pundit, says of her ex-husband, "He has spent more money on baby equipment for his new baby than he spent on our two kids during their entire childhood." Shirley is sharp-tongued about her ex's favoritism, but she is a firm believer that God will make good use of her circumstances. "I think we as Christians are called to forgiveness. I try to model that for the boys. Sure, I sometimes want to rearrange his face when he debits my child support, but I can usually grin and bear it with God's help.**

Sure, I sometimes want to rearrange his face when he debits my child support, but I can usually grin and bear it with God's help.

Abram & Hagar in Scripture

Genesis 16:1-15, 21:8-21

[1]Now Sarai, Abram's wife, had borne him no children. But she had an Egyptian maidservant named Hagar; [2]so she said to Abram, "The LORD has kept me from having children. Go, sleep with my maidservant; perhaps I can build a family through her."

Abram agreed to what Sarai said. [3]So after Abram had been living in Canaan ten years, Sarai his wife took her Egyptian maidservant Hagar and gave her to her husband to be his wife. [4]He slept with Hagar, and she conceived.

When she knew she was pregnant, she began to despise her mistress. [5]Then Sarai said to Abram, "You are responsible for the wrong I am suffering. I put my servant in your arms, and now that she knows she is pregnant, she despises me. May the LORD judge between you and me."

[6]"Your servant is in your hands," Abram said. "Do with her whatever you think best." Then Sarai mistreated Hagar; so she fled from her.

[7]The angel of the LORD found Hagar near a spring in the desert; it was the spring that is beside the road to Shur. [8]And he said, "Hagar, servant of Sarai, where have you come from, and where are you going?"

"I'm running away from my mistress Sarai," she answered.

[9]Then the angel of the LORD told her, "Go back to your mistress and submit to her." [10]The angel added, "I will so increase your descendants that they will be too numerous to count."

[11]The angel of the LORD also said to her:

"You are now with child and you will have a son.

You shall name him Ishmael, for the LORD has heard of your misery. [12]He will be a wild donkey of a man; his hand will be against everyone and everyone's hand against him, and he will live in hostility toward all his brothers."

¹³She gave this name to the LORD who spoke to her: "You are the God who sees me," for she said, "I have now seen the One who sees me." ¹⁴That is why the well was called Beer Lahai Roi; it is still there, between Kadesh and Bered.

¹⁵So Hagar bore Abram a son, and Abram gave the name Ishmael to the son she had borne.

¹⁶Abram was eighty-six years old when Hagar bore him Ishmael.

Genesis 21:8-21

⁸The child grew and was weaned, and on the day Isaac was weaned Abraham held a great feast. ⁹But Sarah saw that the son whom Hagar the Egyptian had borne to Abraham was mocking, ¹⁰and she said to Abraham, "Get rid of that slave woman and her son, for that slave woman's son will never share in the inheritance with my son Isaac."

¹¹The matter distressed Abraham greatly because it concerned his son. ¹²But God said to him, "Do not be so distressed about the boy and your maidservant. Listen to whatever Sarah tells you, because it is through Isaac that your offspring will be reckoned. ¹³I will make the son of the maidservant into a nation also, because he is your offspring."

¹⁴Early the next morning Abraham took some food and a skin of water and gave them to Hagar. He set them on her shoulders and then sent her off with the boy. She went on her way and wandered in the desert of Beersheba.

¹⁵When the water in the skin was gone, she put the boy under one of the bushes. ¹⁶Then she went off and sat down nearby, about a bowshot away, for she thought, "I cannot watch the boy die." And as she sat there nearby, she began to sob.

¹⁷God heard the boy crying, and the angel of God called to Hagar from heaven and said to her, "What is the matter, Hagar? Do not be afraid; God has heard the boy crying as he lies there. ¹⁸Lift the boy up and take him by the hand, for I will make him into a great nation."

¹⁹Then God opened her eyes and she saw a well of water. So she went and filled the skin with water and gave the boy a drink.

²⁰God was with the boy as he grew up. He lived in the desert and became an archer. ²¹While he was living in the Desert of Paran, his mother got a wife for him from Egypt.

Love Stories From the Bible

Rebekah & Isaac

REBEKAH & ISAAC:
KINDNESS HAS CONSEQUENCES.

REBEKAH & ISAAC

Rebekah, the daughter of Betheul and great-niece of Abraham, was a beautiful virgin living in a backwater town called Haran. One evening she went to the community well for water and her life changed dramatically. Eliezer, Abraham's servant, had been sent to Haran in search of just the right girl for Isaac. Rebekah's kindness to Eliezer made her stand out as the mate for Isaac. This young woman walked her talk. She did not simply pop a top on a can of Diet Coke; she watered camels in the hot Middle Eastern sun.

The marriage went fairly well until the children came and then there was favoritism resulting in Jacob's getting Esau's blessing. It seems Rebekah had narrowed down her kindness, the very quality that had made her such a standout.

Love Lesson 5 **Kindness, and its fraternal twin, thoughtfulness, won the day and the mate for my friend Patricia, a California professor. Reaching her forties with no significant other, she decided to take the energy off her personal quest for a life mate and to honor an elderly friend by giving a huge party for that friend's 80th birthday. It was a true labor of love.**

Patricia spent months selecting menus, writing personal notes to grandchildren, and arranging accommodations for out-of-town guests. One of the out-of-towners was a Robert Redford clone named

Ron, who fell under Patricia's charm because she had been so kind to his grandmother. They wed several months later.

Patricia is always eager to tell others that she found her soul mate when she ceased putting all of her energy into the quest for her personal happiness.

Kindness, and its fraternal twin, thoughtfulness, won the day

Rebekah & Isaac in Scripture
Genesis 24:1-66

[1]Abraham was now old and well advanced in years, and the LORD had blessed him in every way. [2]He said to the chief servant in his household, the one in charge of all that he had, "Put your hand under my thigh. [3]I want you to swear by the LORD, the God of heaven and the God of earth, that you will not get a wife for my son from the daughters of the Canaanites, among whom I am living, [4]but will go to my country and my own relatives and get a wife for my son Isaac."

[5]The servant asked him, "What if the woman is unwilling to come back with me to this land? Shall I then take your son back to the country you came from?"

[6]"Make sure that you do not take my son back there," Abraham said. [7]"The LORD, the God of heaven, who brought me out of my father's household and my native land and who spoke to me and promised me on oath, saying, 'To your offspring I will give this land' — he will send his angel before you so that you can get a wife for my son from there. [8]If the woman is unwilling to come back with you, then you will be released from this oath of mine. Only do not take my son back there." [9]So the servant put his hand under the thigh of his master Abraham and swore an oath to him concerning this matter.

[10]Then the servant took ten of his master's camels and left, taking with him all kinds of good things from his master. He set out for Aram Naharaim and made his way to the town of Nahor. [11]He had the camels kneel down near the well outside the town; it was toward evening, the time the women go out to draw water.

[12]Then he prayed, "O LORD, God of my master Abraham, give me success today, and show kindness to my master Abraham. [13]See, I am standing beside this spring,

and the daughters of the townspeople are coming out to draw water. [14]May it be that when I say to a girl, 'Please let down your jar that I may have a drink,' and she says, 'Drink, and I'll water your camels too' — let her be the one you have chosen for your servant Isaac. By this I will know that you have shown kindness to my master."

[15]Before he had finished praying, Rebekah came out with her jar on her shoulder. She was the daughter of Bethuel son of Milcah, who was the wife of Abraham's brother Nahor.

[16]The girl was very beautiful, a virgin; no man had ever lain with her. She went down to the spring, filled her jar and came up again.

[17]The servant hurried to meet her and said, "Please give me a little water from your jar."

[18]"Drink, my lord," she said, and quickly lowered the jar to her hands and gave him a drink.

[19]After she had given him a drink, she said, "I'll draw water for your camels too, until they have finished drinking." [20]So she quickly emptied her jar into the trough, ran back to the well to draw more water, and drew enough for all his camels. [21]Without saying a word, the man watched her closely to learn whether or not the LORD had made his journey successful.

[22]When the camels had finished drinking, the man took out a gold nose ring weighing a beka and two gold bracelets weighing ten shekels. [23]Then he asked, "Whose daughter are you? Please tell me, is there room in your father's house for us to spend the night?"

[24]She answered him, "I am the daughter of Bethuel, the son that Milcah bore to Nahor."

[25]And she added, "We have plenty of straw and fodder, as well as room for you to spend the night."

²⁶Then the man bowed down and worshiped the LORD, ²⁷saying, "Praise be to the LORD, the God of my master Abraham, who has not abandoned his kindness and faithfulness to my master. As for me, the LORD has led me on the journey to the house of my master's relatives."

²⁸The girl ran and told her mother's household about these things. ²⁹Now Rebekah had a brother named Laban, and he hurried out to the man at the spring. ³⁰As soon as he had seen the nose ring, and the bracelets on his sister's arms, and had heard Rebekah tell what the man said to her, he went out to the man and found him standing by the camels near the spring. ³¹"Come, you who are blessed by the LORD," he said. "Why are you standing out here? I have prepared the house and a place for the camels."

³²So the man went to the house, and the camels were unloaded. Straw and fodder were brought for the camels, and water for him and his men to wash their feet. ³³Then food was set before him, but he said, "I will not eat until I have told you what I have to say."

"Then tell us," [Laban] said.

³⁴So he said, "I am Abraham's servant. ³⁵The LORD has blessed my master abundantly, and he has become wealthy. He has given him sheep and cattle, silver and gold, menservants and maidservants, and camels and donkeys. ³⁶My master's wife Sarah has borne him a son in her old age, and he has given him everything he owns. ³⁷And my master made me swear an oath, and said, 'You must not get a wife for my son from the daughters of the Canaanites, in whose land I live, ³⁸but go to my father's family and to my own clan, and get a wife for my son.'

³⁹"Then I asked my master, 'What if the woman will not come back with me?'

⁴⁰"He replied, 'The LORD, before whom I have walked, will send his angel with you and make your journey a success, so that you can get a wife for my son

from my own clan and from my father's family. ⁴¹Then, when you go to my clan, you will be released from my oath even if they refuse to give her to you — you will be released from my oath.'

⁴²"When I came to the spring today, I said, 'O LORD, God of my master Abraham, if you will, please grant success to the journey on which I have come. ⁴³See, I am standing beside this spring; if a maiden comes out to draw water and I say to her, "Please let me drink a little water from your jar," ⁴⁴and if she says to me, "Drink, and I'll draw water for your camels too," let her be the one the LORD has chosen for my master's son.'

⁴⁵"Before I finished praying in my heart, Rebekah came out, with her jar on her shoulder. She went down to the spring and drew water, and I said to her, 'Please give me a drink.'

⁴⁶"She quickly lowered her jar from her shoulder and said, 'Drink, and I'll water your camels too.' So I drank, and she watered the camels also.

⁴⁷"I asked her, 'Whose daughter are you?'

"She said, 'The daughter of Bethuel son of Nahor, whom Milcah bore to him.'

"Then I put the ring in her nose and the bracelets on her arms, ⁴⁸and I bowed down and worshiped the LORD. I praised the LORD, the God of my master Abraham, who had led me on the right road to get the granddaughter of my master's brother for his son. ⁴⁹Now if you will show kindness and faithfulness to my master, tell me; and if not, tell me, so I may know which way to turn."

⁵⁰Laban and Bethuel answered, "This is from the LORD; we can say nothing to you one way or the other. ⁵¹Here is Rebekah; take her and go, and let her become the wife of your master's son, as the LORD has directed."

⁵²When Abraham's servant heard what they said, he bowed down to the ground before the LORD. ⁵³Then the servant brought out gold and silver jewelry

and articles of clothing and gave them to Rebekah; he also gave costly gifts to her brother and to her mother. ⁵⁴Then he and the men who were with him ate and drank and spent the night there.

When they got up the next morning, he said, "Send me on my way to my master."

⁵⁵But her brother and her mother replied, "Let the girl remain with us ten days or so; then you may go."

⁵⁶But he said to them, "Do not detain me, now that the LORD has granted success to my journey. Send me on my way so I may go to my master."

⁵⁷Then they said, "Let's call the girl and ask her about it." ⁵⁸So they called Rebekah and asked her, "Will you go with this man?"

"I will go," she said.

⁵⁹So they sent their sister Rebekah on her way, along with her nurse and Abraham's servant and his men. ⁶⁰And they blessed Rebekah and said to her,

"Our sister, may you increase to thousands upon thousands; may your offspring possess the gates of their enemies."

⁶¹Then Rebekah and her maids got ready and mounted their camels and went back with the man. So the servant took Rebekah and left.

⁶²Now Isaac had come from Beer Lahai Roi, for he was living in the Negev. ⁶³He went out to the field one evening to meditate, and as he looked up, he saw camels approaching. ⁶⁴Rebekah also looked up and saw Isaac. She got down from her camel ⁶⁵and asked the servant, "Who is that man in the field coming to meet us?"

"He is my master," the servant answered. So she took her veil and covered herself.

⁶⁶Then the servant told Isaac all he had done. ⁶⁷Isaac brought her into the tent of his mother Sarah, and he married Rebekah. So she became his wife, and he loved her; and Isaac was comforted after his mother's death.

Love Stories From the Bible

Rachel & Jacob

RACHEL & JACOB:
GOD GIVES US THE POWER
TO DEAL WITH DISAPPOINTMENT.

RACHEL & JACOB

Jacob was the original starry-eyed, love-struck, callow youth. Running away from his brother Esau, Jacob arrived in the town of Haran looking for his uncle Laban.

At the community well, he met Rachel, and just as in Ernest Hemmingway's novels, the earth moved. Unfortunately for Jacob, the well in Haran was not exactly equivalent of a modern-day single's bar. He was centuries away from scoring cell phone numbers, matching astrological signs and other forms of courtship connection. Instead, he existed in an economy that demanded a price for his bride-to-be. Undeterred, the love-smitten young man worked seven years to earn Rachel. One night after an elaborate feast for the benefit of his father-in-law to be, he was finally given the man's daughter's hand in marriage. But there was a major hitch in getting hitched. It seems that Jewish custom prohibited a younger sister from marrying before her old sister tied the knot, a tangled complication that Rachel's father had failed to make clear. So the father gave Jacob Leah, Rachel's older sister. Poor Jacob discovered the bait and switch only after the wedding. Crushed with disappointment, he didn't call his attorney. Instead, he gallantly and faithfully worked for seven more years for Rachel. After all, her older sister was married (technically), and now Rachel was available (sort of). Sticky situation, with all sorts of in-law issues.

Love Lesson 6   **Besides the obvious Caveat Emptor (Let the Buyer Beware!), I have learned that life isn't always fair. In fact, it seldom is. I** have also learned that some things just take longer than others (a test of patience made more intense by our fast-paced world). This lesson served me well when I was first divorced. Assuming our 18-year marriage was made in heaven, I was profoundly shocked when my beloved husband requested that it end on earth. I prayed he would return. He did not. I describe this experience as the scene in the movie where Indiana Jones rips the beating heart out of a man and shows it to him before he drops dead on the ground. In my case, however, I didn't die. And it was a good thing. Seven years later, I married again, having found a soul mate whose spiritual journey paralleled my own. In my experience, disappointment is a type of crucifixion but, as the good book promises, there is also resurrection.

In my experience, disappointment is a type of crucifixion but, as the good book promises, there is also resurrection.

Rachel & Jacob in Scripture

Genesis 29:1-27

[1]Then Jacob continued on his journey and came to the land of the eastern peoples. [2]There he saw a well in the field, with three flocks of sheep lying near it because the flocks were watered from that well. The stone over the mouth of the well was large. [3]When all the flocks were gathered there, the shepherds would roll the stone away from the well's mouth and water the sheep. Then they would return the stone to its place over the mouth of the well.

[4]Jacob asked the shepherds, "My brothers, where are you from?" "We're from Haran," they replied.

[5]He said to them, "Do you know Laban, Nahor's grandson?" "Yes, we know him," they answered.

[6]Then Jacob asked them, "Is he well?" "Yes, he is," they said, "and here comes his daughter Rachel with the sheep."

[7]"Look," he said, "the sun is still high; it is not time for the flocks to be gathered. Water the sheep and take them back to pasture."

[8]"We can't," they replied, "until all the flocks are gathered and the stone has been rolled away from the mouth of the well. Then we will water the sheep."

[9]While he was still talking with them, Rachel came with her father's sheep, for she was a shepherdess. [10]When Jacob saw Rachel daughter of Laban, his mother's brother, and Laban's sheep, he went over and rolled the stone away from the mouth of the well and watered his uncle's sheep. [11]Then Jacob kissed Rachel and began to weep aloud. [12]He had told Rachel that he was a relative of her father and a son of Rebekah. So she ran and told her father.

[13]As soon as Laban heard the news about Jacob, his sister's son, he hurried to meet him. He embraced him and kissed him and brought him to his home, and

there Jacob told him all these things. [14]Then Laban said to him, "You are my own flesh and blood." After Jacob had stayed with him for a whole month, [15]Laban said to him, "Just because you are a relative of mine, should you work for me for nothing? Tell me what your wages should be."

[16]Now Laban had two daughters; the name of the older was Leah, and the name of the younger was Rachel. [17]Leah had weak eyes, but Rachel was lovely in form, and beautiful. [18]Jacob was in love with Rachel and said, "I'll work for you seven years in return for your younger daughter Rachel."

[19]Laban said, "It's better that I give her to you than to some other man. Stay here with me." [20]So Jacob served seven years to get Rachel, but they seemed like only a few days to him because of his love for her.

[21]Then Jacob said to Laban, "Give me my wife. My time is completed, and I want to lie with her."

[22]So Laban brought together all the people of the place and gave a feast. [23]But when evening came, he took his daughter Leah and gave her to Jacob, and Jacob lay with her. [24]And Laban gave his servant girl Zilpah to his daughter as her maid-servant.

[25]When morning came, there was Leah! So Jacob said to Laban, "What is this you have done to me? I served you for Rachel, didn't I? Why have you deceived me?"

[26]Laban replied, "It is not our custom here to give the younger daughter in marriage before the older one. [27]Finish this daughter's bridal week; then we will give you the younger one also, in return for another seven years of work."

Love Stories From the Bible

Tamar & Judah

TAMAR & JUDAH:
TENACITY IS A GIFT FROM GOD.

TAMAR & JUDAH

Now here is a story that had enough intrigue for even the most jaded adolescent. Tamar, a Canaanite, marries Er, the oldest son of Judah and Shuah, Canaanites also. Er dies. According to Hebrew law, Tamar marries the next son in the family so that he could have a child for the deceased. No luck. The second son dies also. Tamar, who is beginning to feel like the black widow, technically gets the third son but the father is reluctant to make the match. When the mother dies, Tamar dresses up like a harlot and sits in a spot the father will have to pass. The father drops in for a dalliance. Later he is horrified to learn that Tamar was the harlot. Nevertheless, twin sons were born of the union. One of them, Pharez, was an ancestor of Jesus.

Love Lesson 7 **One wise revival preacher who held forth on this passage said that the Tamar and Judah episode meant that both Jews and Gentiles would be part of Jesus' lineage and ministry. He also said that the passage demonstrated the fact God could override evil for His own good purpose.**

That overriding power certainly seems true in my colleague Louise's life. After many years of marriage, her husband left her with four children and an indwelling sense of failure. When the children reached adulthood, she used her sense of loss and failure—which remained her companion— as a bridge into a unique ministry. Now,

when someone asks her how she is spending a weekend, it is not unusual to hear this octogenarian say, "I'm going to jail." Petite and indus- trious, Louise heads up many of the home-baked cookie contributions for KAIROS, a nationally recognized prison ministry. Her hope is that the ministry will spread to all major prisons in Florida. Like Tamar, Louise is holding tenaciously to her goals.

God overrides evil for His own good purpose.

Tamar & Judah in Scripture

Genesis 38:1-30

[1]At that time, Judah left his brothers and went down to stay with a man of Adullam named Hirah. [2]There Judah met the daughter of a Canaanite man named Shua. He married her and lay with her; [3]she became pregnant and gave birth to a son, who was named Er. [4]She conceived again and gave birth to a son and named him Onan. [5]She gave birth to still another son and named him Shelah. It was at Kezib that she gave birth to him.

[6]Judah got a wife for Er, his firstborn, and her name was Tamar. [7]But Er, Judah's firstborn, was wicked in the LORD's sight; so the LORD put him to death.

[8]Then Judah said to Onan, "Lie with your brother's wife and fulfill your duty to her as a brother-in-law to produce offspring for your brother." [9]But Onan knew that the offspring would not be his; so whenever he lay with his brother's wife, he spilled his semen on the ground to keep from producing offspring for his brother. [10]What he did was wicked in the LORD's sight; so he put him to death also.

[11]Judah then said to his daughter-in-law Tamar, "Live as a widow in your father's house until my son Shelah grows up." For he thought, "He may die too, just like his brothers." So Tamar went to live in her father's house.

[12]After a long time Judah's wife, the daughter of Shua, died. When Judah had recovered from his grief, he went up to Timnah, to the men who were shearing his sheep, and his friend Hirah the Adullamite went with him.

[13]When Tamar was told, "Your father-in-law is on his way to Timnah to shear his sheep," [14]she took off her widow's clothes, covered herself with a veil to disguise herself, and then sat down at the entrance to Enaim, which is on the road to Timnah. For she saw that, though Shelah had now grown up, she had not been given to him as his wife.

¹⁵When Judah saw her, he thought she was a prostitute, for she had covered her face. ¹⁶Not realizing that she was his daughter-in-law, he went over to her by the roadside and said, "Come now, let me sleep with you." "And what will you give me to sleep with you?" she asked.

¹⁷"I'll send you a young goat from my flock," he said. "Will you give me something as a pledge until you send it?" she asked.

¹⁸He said, "What pledge should I give you?"

"Your seal and its cord, and the staff in your hand," she answered. So he gave them to her and slept with her, and she became pregnant by him. ¹⁹After she left, she took off her veil and put on her widow's clothes again.

²⁰Meanwhile Judah sent the young goat by his friend the Adullamite in order to get his pledge back from the woman, but he did not find her. ²¹He asked the men who lived there, "Where is the shrine prostitute who was beside the road at Enaim?"

"There hasn't been any shrine prostitute here," they said.

²²So he went back to Judah and said, "I didn't find her. Besides, the men who lived there said, 'There hasn't been any shrine prostitute here.'"

²³Then Judah said, "Let her keep what she has, or we will become a laughing-stock. After all, I did send her this young goat, but you didn't find her."

²⁴About three months later Judah was told, "Your daughter-in-law Tamar is guilty of prostitution, and as a result she is now pregnant." Judah said, "Bring her out and have her burned to death!"

²⁵As she was being brought out, she sent a message to her father-in-law. "I am pregnant by the man who owns these," she said. And she added, "See if you recognize whose seal and cord and staff these are."

²⁶Judah recognized them and said, "She is more righteous than I, since I wouldn't give her to my son Shelah." And he did not sleep with her again.

²⁷When the time came for her to give birth, there were twin boys in her womb. ²⁸As she was giving birth, one of them put out his hand; so the midwife took a scarlet thread and tied it on his wrist and said, "This one came out first." ²⁹But when he drew back his hand, his brother came out, and she said, "So this is how you have broken out!" And he was named Perez. ³⁰Then his brother, who had the scarlet thread on his wrist, came out and he was given the name Zerah.

Love Stories From the Bible

Moses & Zipporah

MOSES & ZIPPORAH:
MIXED MARRIAGE IS A DIFFICULT
PROPOSITION.

MOSES & ZIPPORAH

As a biblical storyteller once quipped, Moses and Zipporah are a pair that takes the fun out of dysfunctional. Their relationship began in bliss and ended in blame. They met— as so many biblical couples do— at a well. Zipporah, the eldest of the seven daughters of Jethro, was drawing water, and Moses, the suave Egyptian, helped her with the water, but failed to mention the fact that he was wanted for murder in Egypt.

Because of his help at the watering station, Moses was invited to meet the family. Jethro, Zipporah's dad, liked the young man and let him stay. He lived with them for some time and then married Zipporah, ignoring the fact that she was a Midian who did not share his values. They had two sons, Gerhom and Eliezer. As with many a mixed marriage, each individual tried to honor his or her own sacred customs. On occasion, Moses found himself acting against the sacred tradition of Israel. For example, he did not circumcise Eliezer. God was not happy over this omission and as a sign of His displeasure, struck Moses down with a deadly disease. To placate Yahweh, Zipporah performed a do-it-yourself circumcision on Eliezer and flung the bloody foreskin at Moses saying, *"Surely you are a bridegroom of blood to me"* (Exodus 4:25).

Their marriage did not survive this experience. Moses went to Egypt and Zipporah returned to Midia. As a leader, Moses micromanaged the Israelites, acting as judge all day every day. Indeed, Jethro, his father-in-law, who went to try and repair his daughter's marriage, said *"What you are doing is not good. You and these people who come to you will only wear yourselves out. The* work is too heavy for you cannot handle it alone" (Exodus 18:18). Then Jethro advised Moses: "*Select capable men from all the people and appoint them as officials over thousands, hundreds, fifties and tens*" (Exodus 18:21).

Moses listened to his father-in-law and did everything he said, but it was too late to repair the marriage. Zipporah disappeared without comment from the history of the Jewish people in which her husband figured so prominently. The "little sparrow," as her name translates into, flew into historical oblivion.

Love Lesson 8   **Virginia, a divorced mother of two, relates to the Moses /Zipporah story. She married a very successful man who was an agnostic. Initially, she thought he was interested in Eastern religions because of his "Honk if you love Buddha"** *Marriage is tough enough without adding the extra burden of different faiths.* **bumper sticker, but he was a true agnostic, someone who thought God was unknowable. At first there was no problem with Virginia worshipping at First Baptist on Sunday while he watched the golf channel. After the children** **were born, however, the religious question became more pressing. The father wanted the children to go to church only if they chose to go. For a four- and a seven-year-old staying with Dad, eating frozen pot pies, and being allowed to use the remote were more appealing than suiting up for Sunday school. The** marriage ran ashore on the rocks of radically different religious outlooks. The relationship lesson here appears to be a simple one. Marriage is tough enough without adding the extra burden of different faiths.

Moses and Zipporah in Scripture

Exodus 2:21-22

2:21Moses agreed to stay with the man, who gave his daughter Zipporah to Moses in marriage. 22Zipporah gave birth to a son, and Moses named him Gershom, saying, "I have become an alien in a foreign land."

Exodus 4:25-26

25But Zipporah took a flint knife, cut off her son's foreskin and touched [Moses'] feet with it. "Surely you are a bridegroom of blood to me," she said. 26So the LORD let him alone. (At that time she said "bridegroom of blood," referring to circumcision.)

Love Stories From the Bible

Deborah & Lappidoth

DEBORAH & LAPPIDOTH:
GOD'S WOMEN CAN
SERVE AS JUST JUDGES.

DEBORAH & LAPPIDOTH

Growing Up in the 1950s when most of the grown women I knew were moms, the story of Deborah and Lappidoth seemed puzzling. Now, the story makes a little more sense.

This was a relationship tale in which the woman behind her man leapfrogged in front of him. Deborah was the only woman judge in the Bible, one of the leaders of Israel in the period before the kings. According to Rhonda Kelley, author of *Life Lessons from Women in the Bible*, Deborah's name means *bee* in Hebrew.

Every time I read that factoid, I am reminded that a wise friend once told me, *"Bees can't fly. Their wingspan-to-fuselage ratio is wrong. But bees don't know about this, so they fly."* Evidently, Deborah lived up to her name. She didn't give much credence to the fact that the vocational deck was stacked against her. Surely she knew that women were generally restricted to home and hearth in ancient Israel. She simply followed God's plan for her life and became the Condoleezza Rice /Sandra Day O'Connor of her era, advising generals and holding court under Deborah's Palm in the hills of Ephraim.

Readers of the Bible know very little about her biography except for her marital status, which is documented in Judges 4:4. She is duly noted as the wife of Lappidoth. So who was Lappidoth? What was their chemistry as a couple? One can only assume that Lappidoth was a godly man who saw how God was using his wife. He must have been a man of NASCAR driver confidence, because it would take such confidence to withstand the jibes and comments of his buddies in a society as patriarchal as ancient Israel.

Love Lesson 9 Francis, one of the first women priests in her denomination, draws courage and energy from Deborah's story. "Here was a woman who moved boldly into the all male world of leadership, and yet did not lose her God-given femininity. She was referred to as a mother of Israel. She had to have a companion who affirmed her and who helped her reach her goals of direction and protection for her people. Breaking the leadership glass ceiling is too lonely unless someone close to you understands your commitment to a larger purpose."

Lappidoth's name means torches in Hebrew. That fits. He provided the clarity and the warmth for Deborah to accomplish her demanding tasks. As Rhonda Kelley says, "Christian women today are challenged to leave a legacy of just leadership that always follows God's direction."

Christian women today are challenged to leave a legacy of just leadership that always follows God's direction.

Deborah & Lappidoth in Scripture

Judges 4:4-16

⁴Deborah, a prophetess, the wife of Lappidoth, was leading Israel at that time. ⁵She held court under the Palm of Deborah between Ramah and Bethel in the hill country of Ephraim, and the Israelites came to her to have their disputes decided. ⁶She sent for Barak son of Abinoam from Kedesh in Naphtali and said to him, "The LORD, the God of Israel, commands you: 'Go, take with you ten thousand men of Naphtali and Zebulun and lead the way to Mount Tabor. ⁷I will lure Sisera, the commander of Jabin's army, with his chariots and his troops to the Kishon River and give him into your hands.'"

⁸Barak said to her, "If you go with me, I will go; but if you don't go with me, I won't go."

⁹"Very well," Deborah said, "I will go with you. But because of the way you are going about this, the honor will not be yours, for the LORD will hand Sisera over to a woman." So Deborah went with Barak to Kedesh, ¹⁰where he summoned Zebulun and Naphtali. Ten thousand men followed him, and Deborah also went with him.

¹¹Now Heber the Kenite had left the other Kenites, the descendants of Hobab, Moses' brother-in-law, and pitched his tent by the great tree in Zaanannim near Kedesh.

¹²When they told Sisera that Barak son of Abinoam had gone up to Mount Tabor, ¹³Sisera gathered together his nine hundred iron chariots and all the men with him, from Harosheth Haggoyim to the Kishon River.

¹⁴Then Deborah said to Barak, "Go! This is the day the LORD has given Sisera into your hands. Has not the LORD gone ahead of you?" So Barak went down Mount Tabor, followed by ten thousand men. ¹⁵At Barak's advance, the LORD

routed Sisera and all his chariots and army by the sword, and Sisera abandoned his chariot and fled on foot. ¹⁶But Barak pursued the chariots and army as far as Harosheth Haggoyim. All the troops of Sisera fell by the sword; not a man was left.

Love Stories From the Bible

Hannah & Elkanah

HANNAH & ELKANAH:
ALL THINGS ARE POSSIBLE TO THOSE
WHO LOVE THE LORD.

HANNAH & ELKANAH

In a recent magazine cartoon the pastor said, "In the Old Testament a man could have as many wives as he could afford." And a jaded parishioner answered, "Kinda like today!" Irony aside, Hannah and Elkanah were part of a polygamous family. Hannah, wife of Elkanah the priest, was childless and she was constantly reminded of this fact by Elkanah's second wife Peninnah, who had produced several children and never missed an opportunity to remind Hannah of her own barrenness. Perhaps Peninnah's venomous reminders stemmed from the fact that Elkanah was obvious in his favoritism toward Hannah. This was shown in 1 Samuel 1:5, *"But to Hannah he gave a double portion because he loved her and the Lord had closed her womb."* Priest though he was, Elkanah was what Southerners refer to as a *Bubba* in the arena of emotions. He was oblivious to Hannah's pain. Like Dick Cavett, a 1980s T.V. personality, he was certain that HE was the blessed event in his family. Seeing her downhearted, he wailed, *"Don't I mean more to you than ten sons?"* (1 Samuel 1:8). Hannah gave that remark the silence it deserved.

Hannah had Melanie Wilkes' patience and compassion. She never responded negatively to Peninnah's jabs. She prayed without ceasing for a son, promising God that she would give the child to the priesthood if she could conceive. Ironically, her intense silent prayer of supplication was misinterpreted by Eli, an elderly priest who thought Hannah's wordless prayer was the result of too much wine. Shocked and saddened, Hannah convinced Eli that she was merely fervid in her desire for a child to give to God. Eli lightened her heart when he said, *"Go in peace and may the God of Israel grant what you have been waiting for"* (1 Samuel 1:17).

So Hannah went in peace, and the peace changed to joy when she discovered that she was pregnant. She named the little boy Samuel, which means "asked of the Lord." When she weaned the boy, she took him to the house of the Lord to stay forever. Hannah visited him once a year and gave him another hand-stitched robe.

Love Lesson 10 "Hannah provides a model of the possible for me," says Tory, a young mother. "I went through a period when I could not conceive, and I was not the model of patience. Also, my husband was married once before and just the knowledge that he and his ex-wife had no difficult conceiving really hurt me. I felt defective. I tried to pray, but all I wanted to do was log on to the Internet and visit chat rooms with other women who were having trouble. It took a good friend of mine to direct me to Hannah's grace-filled patience as an alternative to my frenetic despair. God does answer prayers. Jeremy (her two-year-old son) is my daily reminder of that.

Hannah & Elkanah in Scripture
1 Samuel 1:1-28, 1 Samuel 2:1-21

¹There was a certain man from Ramathaim, a Zuphite from the hill country of Ephraim, whose name was Elkanah son of Jeroham, the son of Elihu, the son of Tohu, the son of Zuph, an Ephraimite. ²He had two wives; one was called Hannah and the other Peninnah. Peninnah had children, but Hannah had none.

³Year after year this man went up from his town to worship and sacrifice to the LORD Almighty at Shiloh, where Hophni and Phinehas, the two sons of Eli, were priests of the LORD. ⁴Whenever the day came for Elkanah to sacrifice, he would give portions of the meat to his wife Peninnah and to all her sons and daughters. ⁵But to Hannah he gave a double portion because he loved her, and the LORD had closed her womb. ⁶And because the LORD had closed her womb, her rival kept provoking her in order to irritate her. ⁷This went on year after year. Whenever Hannah went up to the house of the LORD, her rival provoked her till she wept and would not eat. ⁸Elkanah her husband would say to her, "Hannah, why are you weeping? Why don't you eat? Why are you downhearted? Don't I mean more to you than ten sons?"

⁹Once when they had finished eating and drinking in Shiloh, Hannah stood up. Now Eli the priest was sitting on a chair by the doorpost of the LORD's temple. ¹⁰In bitterness of soul Hannah wept much and prayed to the LORD. ¹¹And she made a vow, saying, "O LORD Almighty, if you will only look upon your servant's misery and remember me, and not forget your servant but give her a son, then I will give him to the LORD for all the days of his life, and no razor will ever be used on his head."

¹²As she kept on praying to the LORD, Eli observed her mouth. ¹³Hannah was praying in her heart, and her lips were moving but her voice was not heard. Eli

thought she was drunk 14and said to her, "How long will you keep on getting drunk? Get rid of your wine."

15"Not so, my lord," Hannah replied, "I am a woman who is deeply troubled. I have not been drinking wine or beer; I was pouring out my soul to the LORD. 16Do not take your servant for a wicked woman; I have been praying here out of my great anguish and grief."

17Eli answered, "Go in peace, and may the God of Israel grant you what you have asked of him."

18She said, "May your servant find favor in your eyes." Then she went her way and ate something, and her face was no longer downcast.

19Early the next morning they arose and worshiped before the LORD and then went back to their home at Ramah. Elkanah lay with Hannah his wife, and the LORD remembered her. 20So in the course of time Hannah conceived and gave birth to a son. She named him Samuel, saying, "Because I asked the LORD for him."

21When the man Elkanah went up with all his family to offer the annual sacrifice to the LORD and to fulfill his vow, 22Hannah did not go. She said to her husband, "After the boy is weaned, I will take him and present him before the LORD, and he will live there always."

23"Do what seems best to you," Elkanah her husband told her. "Stay here until you have weaned him; only may the LORD make good his word." So the woman stayed at home and nursed her son until she had weaned him.

24After he was weaned, she took the boy with her, young as he was, along with a three-year-old bull, an ephah of flour and a skin of wine, and brought him to the house of the LORD at Shiloh. 25When they had slaughtered the bull, they brought the boy to Eli, 26and she said to him, "As surely as you live, my lord, I am the woman who stood here beside you praying to the LORD. 27I prayed for this child, and the LORD has granted me what I asked of him. 28So now I give him to the LORD. For his whole life he will be given over to the LORD." And he worshiped the LORD there.

1 Samuel 2:1-21

[1]Then Hannah prayed and said:

"My heart rejoices in the LORD; in the LORD my horn is lifted high. My mouth boasts over my enemies, for I delight in your deliverance.

[2]"There is no one holy like the LORD; there is no one besides you; there is no Rock like our God.

[3]"Do not keep talking so proudly or let your mouth speak such arrogance, for the LORD is a God who knows, and by him deeds are weighed.

[4]"The bows of the warriors are broken, but those who stumbled are armed with strength. [5]Those who were full hire themselves out for food, but those who were hungry hunger no more. She who was barren has borne seven children, but she who has had many sons pines away.

[6]"The LORD brings death and makes alive; he brings down to the grave and raises up. [7]The LORD sends poverty and wealth; he humbles and he exalts. [8]He raises the poor from the dust and lifts the needy from the ash heap; he seats them with princes and has them inherit a throne of honor.

"For the foundations of the earth are the LORD's; upon them he has set the world. [9]He will guard the feet of his saints, but the wicked will be silenced in darkness.

"It is not by strength that one prevails; [10]those who oppose the LORD will be shattered. He will thunder against them from heaven; the LORD will judge the ends of the earth.

"He will give strength to his king and exalt the horn of his anointed."

[11]Then Elkanah went home to Ramah, but the boy ministered before the LORD under Eli the priest.

[12]Eli's sons were wicked men; they had no regard for the LORD. [13]Now it was the practice of the priests with the people that whenever anyone offered a sacrifice and while the meat was being boiled, the servant of the priest would come with a three-pronged fork in his hand. [14]He would plunge it into the pan or kettle or caldron or pot, and the priest would take for himself whatever the fork brought up. This is how they treated all the Israelites who came to Shiloh. [15]But even before the fat was burned, the servant of the priest would come and say to the man who was sacrificing, "Give the priest some meat to roast; he won't accept boiled meat from you, but only raw."

[16]If the man said to him, "Let the fat be burned up first, and then take whatever you want," the servant would then answer, "No, hand it over now; if you don't, I'll take it by force."

[17]This sin of the young men was very great in the LORD's sight, for they were treating the LORD's offering with contempt.

[18]But Samuel was ministering before the LORD-a boy wearing a linen ephod. [19]Each year his mother made him a little robe and took it to him when she went up with her husband to offer the annual sacrifice. [20]Eli would bless Elkanah and his wife, saying, "May the LORD give you children by this woman to take the place of the one she prayed for and gave to the LORD." Then they would go home. [21]And the LORD was gracious to Hannah; she conceived and gave birth to three sons and two daughters. Meanwhile, the boy Samuel grew up in the presence of the LORD.

Love Stories From the Bible

David & Abigail

DAVID & ABIGAIL:
WISDOM COMES FROM GOD.

DAVID & ABIGAIL

David was a true Rhett Butler figure when he met Abigail. Like the dashing blockade-runner, David was trying to escape another force, King Saul's army. Abigail— according to 1 Samuel 25:3— was an "*intelligent and beautiful woman married to a Calebite (who) was surly and mean in his dealings.*" His name was Nabal. In case the reader misses the mismatch, Nabal's name, according to Abigail in a later verse, means *fool.*

And fool he was. Nabal conveniently ignored the fact that David had done him an earlier good service. Nabal paid back evil for good, and David was not amused. He lined up to annihilate Nabal's home like General Sherman did Atlanta. He said, "*May God deal with David be it ever so severely if by morning I leave alive one male of all who belong to him!*" (1 Samuel 25:22).

Meanwhile, Abigail lost no time. She packed two hundred loaves of bread and all the fixins on her donkey. She rode into the ravine and headed off David and his men. She bowed to him in a most feminine fashion and then filled his belly with good food and his brain with predictions of success. Later she asked a boon. In 1 Samuel 25:31 she said, "*And when the Lord has brought my master success, remember your servant.*"

And David did remember the beautiful damsel with the great roasted goat sandwiches. He married her after Nabal died of shock from Abigail's adventurous tale. David's delight was obvious in 1 Samuel 2, 5:39," *Praise is to the Lord who has up held my cause against Nabal for treating me with contempt.*" Abigail was also delighted. She ignored the idea of the decent interval between husbands, hopped on her donkey, called her five maids, and went with David's messengers to become one of David's wives.

Love Lesson 11   **What is the life lesson for me in the Abigail story? Strangely enough it has to do with procrastination and connection. Abigail does not procrastinate. When she finds out that Nabal has fatally insulted David, she takes action. She loads the donkey, climbs aboard, and takes off for the hinterland. Once she engages David, she is quick to display the wisdom God has granted her. She asks David to use his God-given rationality, and to abstain from doing something he will later regret. She reminds David that he has trusted God for victory in the past, and he can do it again. She sits in the position of story-keeper for David, calling up the past to illuminate the present.**

Memory is a gift from God, and story keepers are powerful people.

Memory is a gift from God, and story keepers are powerful people. My friend Carolyn, a mental health counselor, uses specific, positive memories to help her clients deal with difficulty. A formal name for this technique is Narrative Therapy. Quite often, she will remind her clients of a time when they have exhibited their God-given abilities to be resilient or compassionate. Attaching the current stressful situation to a productive past experience is a powerful healing tool. In the South it is the duty of good buddies and Ya-Ya sisters to remind one another of their productive coping during times of trial. As one of my father's good pilot buddies said to him when he was trying to cope with increasingly computerized aircraft, "Harry Lee, you plowed behind a mule and you took the controls of a 747. This stuff ain't gonna get ya."

David & Abigail in Scripture

1 Samuel 25:1-42

¹Now Samuel died, and all Israel assembled and mourned for him; and they buried him at his home in Ramah.

Then David moved down into the Desert of Maon. ²A certain man in Maon, who had property there at Carmel, was very wealthy. He had a thousand goats and three thousand sheep, which he was shearing in Carmel. ³His name was Nabal and his wife's name was Abigail. She was an intelligent and beautiful woman, but her husband, a Calebite, was surly and mean in his dealings.

⁴While David was in the desert, he heard that Nabal was shearing sheep. ⁵So he sent ten young men and said to them, "Go up to Nabal at Carmel and greet him in my name. ⁶Say to him: 'Long life to you! Good health to you and your household! And good health to all that is yours!

⁷"'Now I hear that it is sheep-shearing time. When your shepherds were with us, we did not mistreat them, and the whole time they were at Carmel nothing of theirs was missing. ⁸Ask your own servants and they will tell you. Therefore be favorable toward my young men, since we come at a festive time. Please give your servants and your son David whatever you can find for them.'"

⁹When David's men arrived, they gave Nabal this message in David's name. Then they waited.

¹⁰Nabal answered David's servants, "Who is this David? Who is this son of Jesse? Many servants are breaking away from their masters these days. ¹¹Why should I take my bread and water, and the meat I have slaughtered for my shearers, and give it to men coming from who knows where?"

¹²David's men turned around and went back. When they arrived, they reported every word. ¹³David said to his men, "Put on your swords!" So they put

on their swords, and David put on his. About four hundred men went up with David, while two hundred stayed with the supplies.

¹⁴One of the servants told Nabal's wife Abigail: "David sent messengers from the desert to give our master his greetings, but he hurled insults at them. ¹⁵Yet these men were very good to us. They did not mistreat us, and the whole time we were out in the fields near them nothing was missing. ¹⁶Night and day they were a wall around us all the time we were herding our sheep near them. ¹⁷Now think it over and see what you can do, because disaster is hanging over our master and his whole household. He is such a wicked man that no one can talk to him."

¹⁸Abigail lost no time. She took two hundred loaves of bread, two skins of wine, five dressed sheep, five seahs of roasted grain, a hundred cakes of raisins and two hundred cakes of pressed figs, and loaded them on donkeys. ¹⁹Then she told her servants, "Go on ahead; I'll follow you." But she did not tell her husband Nabal.

²⁰As she came riding her donkey into a mountain ravine, there were David and his men descending toward her, and she met them. ²¹David had just said, "It's been useless-all my watching over this fellow's property in the desert so that nothing of his was missing. He has paid me back evil for good. ²²May God deal with David, be it ever so severely, if by morning I leave alive one male of all who belong to him!"

²³When Abigail saw David, she quickly got off her donkey and bowed down before David with her face to the ground. ²⁴She fell at his feet and said: "My lord, let the blame be on me alone. Please let your servant speak to you; hear what your servant has to say. ²⁵May my lord pay no attention to that wicked man Nabal. He is just like his name-his name is Fool, and folly goes with him. But as for me, your servant, I did not see the men my master sent.

²⁶"Now since the LORD has kept you, my master, from bloodshed and from avenging yourself with your own hands, as surely as the LORD lives and as you live, may your enemies and all who intend to harm my master be like Nabal.

²⁷And let this gift, which your servant has brought to my master, be given to the men who follow you. ²⁸Please forgive your servant's offense, for the LORD will certainly make a lasting dynasty for my master, because he fights the LORD's battles. Let no wrongdoing be found in you as long as you live. ²⁹Even though someone is pursuing you to take your life, the life of my master will be bound securely in the bundle of the living by the LORD your God. But the lives of your enemies he will hurl away as from the pocket of a sling. ³⁰When the LORD has done for my master every good thing he promised concerning him and has appointed him leader over Israel, ³¹my master will not have on his conscience the staggering burden of needless bloodshed or of having avenged himself. And when the LORD has brought my master success, remember your servant."

³²David said to Abigail, "Praise be to the LORD, the God of Israel, who has sent you today to meet me. ³³May you be blessed for your good judgment and for keeping me from bloodshed this day and from avenging myself with my own hands. ³⁴Otherwise, as surely as the LORD, the God of Israel, lives, who has kept me from harming you, if you had not come quickly to meet me, not one male belonging to Nabal would have been left alive by daybreak."

³⁵Then David accepted from her hand what she had brought him and said, "Go home in peace. I have heard your words and granted your request."

³⁶When Abigail went to Nabal, he was in the house holding a banquet like that of a king. He was in high spirits and very drunk. So she told him nothing until daybreak. ³⁷Then in the morning, when Nabal was sober, his wife told him all these things, and his heart failed him and he became like a stone. ³⁸About ten days later, the LORD struck Nabal and he died.

³⁹When David heard that Nabal was dead, he said, "Praise be to the LORD, who has upheld my cause against Nabal for treating me with contempt. He has kept his servant from doing wrong and has brought Nabal's wrongdoing down on his own head."

Then David sent word to Abigail, asking her to become his wife. [40]His servants went to Carmel and said to Abigail, "David has sent us to you to take you to become his wife."

[41]She bowed down with her face to the ground and said, "Here is your maidservant, ready to serve you and wash the feet of my master's servants." [42]Abigail quickly got on a donkey and, attended by her five maids, went with David's messengers and became his wife.

Love Stories From the Bible

David & Bathsheba

DAVID & BATHSHEBA:
CONFESSION DOES NOT
REMOVE CONSEQUENCE.

DAVID & BATHSHEBA

Of course, no list of love stories is complete without the pulsating, midlife crisis tale of David and Bathsheba. David, the ruler of all Israel, was a poster boy for kingly excellence. He was a celebrated warrior, an expert in sling-shotting giants, a harpist, a poet, a devoted father and a believer in one true God. One evening as he was strolling around the palace grounds, he spotted Bathsheba bathing. The wife of one of his soldiers, she was definitely a 10. As the late mythologist Joseph Campbell was fond of saying, "lust of the organs" overrode David's better and more kingly judgment. He promptly ordered the damp damsel to the palace boudoir. Bathsheba, perhaps regretting her public bath, had no choice. Defying a king was less a matter of defending one's modesty and more a matter of chancing execution.

The morning after their romp, David sent Bathesheba home. But their tryst was far from over. As David soon discovered, the wild oats he had sown had produced a harvest: Bathsheba was pregnant. In desperation, David gave Bathsheba's husband Uriah a pass home from the front lines of battle, fully expecting that Uriah would sleep with her and cover David's misdeed. Uriah, proving himself to be more a principled leader than his commander-in-chief, slept at the palace door rather than in his own bed. It seemed Uriah just couldn't enjoy himself while his men were still in the trenches.

Ironically, Uriah's noble gesture brought out the worst in David. The king ordered Uriah out of his doorway and back onto the front lines. In a chilling note to Joab, his army commander, David directed him to put Uriah in the most dangerous place, and then to fall back and let him be slaughtered by the enemy (2 Samuel 11:15). Joab carried out this evil deed, and Uriah was slain.

Enter the prophet Nathan, who told David a parable about a poor man whose only ewe was stolen by a rich man. Enraged over the inequity, David pronounced harsh judgment on the felon: the man that hath done this thing shall surely die (2 Samuel 12:7). Facing his own depravity, David became contrite. He repented and was forgiven by God, but—as my grandmother Mimi used to emphasize in her deep Tennessee twang—the consequences of his immoral act remained. David and Bathsheba's child died. His other children remained at war with each other. Amnon, David's eldest son, raped his half-sister Tamar. Absalom publicly slept with his father's concubines and was later murdered by Joab. Solomon, his most famous son, killed a sibling.

Love Lesson 12 **To me, it's the eternal message that confession may not remove consequence. In a time when the word "spin" has moved from the family laundry room to a job description for a presidential press secretary, David's moral dilemmas remind me to be honest when I fail to walk my talk as a woman of faith. Attempted cover-ups only lead to more wreckage on the relationship road. God will meet me more than halfway down that highway if I am absolutely honest and totally repentant. Nevertheless, God will not remove the consequence of my actions. If I break the mirror, I have to sweep up the pieces, and I might get cut by the jagged glass.**

David & Bathsheba in Scripture

2 Samuel 11:2-17

²One evening David got up from his bed and walked around on the roof of the palace. From the roof he saw a woman bathing. The woman was very beautiful, ³and David sent someone to find out about her. The man said, "Isn't this Bathsheba, the daughter of Eliam and the wife of Uriah the Hittite?" ⁴Then David sent messengers to get her. She came to him, and he slept with her. (She had purified herself from her uncleanness.) Then she went back home. ⁵The woman conceived and sent word to David, saying, "I am pregnant."

⁶So David sent this word to Joab: "Send me Uriah the Hittite." And Joab sent him to David. ⁷When Uriah came to him, David asked him how Joab was, how the soldiers were and how the war was going. ⁸Then David said to Uriah, "Go down to your house and wash your feet." So Uriah left the palace, and a gift from the king was sent after him. ⁹But Uriah slept at the entrance to the palace with all his master's servants and did not go down to his house.

¹⁰When David was told, "Uriah did not go home," he asked him, "Haven't you just come from a distance? Why didn't you go home?"

¹¹Uriah said to David, "The ark and Israel and Judah are staying in tents, and my master Joab and my lord's men are camped in the open fields. How could I go to my house to eat and drink and lie with my wife? As surely as you live, I will not do such a thing!"

¹²Then David said to him, "Stay here one more day, and tomorrow I will send you back." So Uriah remained in Jerusalem that day and the next. ¹³At David's invitation, he ate and drank with him, and David made him drunk. But in the evening Uriah went out to sleep on his mat among his master's servants; he did not go home.

[14]In the morning David wrote a letter to Joab and sent it with Uriah. [15]In it he wrote, "Put Uriah in the front line where the fighting is fiercest. Then withdraw from him so he will be struck down and die."

[16]So while Joab had the city under siege, he put Uriah at a place where he knew the strongest defenders were. [17]When the men of the city came out and fought against Joab, some of the men in David's army fell; moreover, Uriah the Hittite died.

Love Stories From the Bible

Tamar & Amnon

TAMAR & AMNON:
GOD IS NOT MOCKED.

TAMAR & AMNON

To many Southern women, the cad-of- the-century award goes to Amnon, King David's oldest son who fixated on his virgin half-sister Tamar. (Now this is not Tamar the Tenacious who bedded her father-in-law in Genesis.) Running some vivid mental movies about the damsel, Amnon grew pale and wan. The plot thickened as his cousin Jonadab came up with a plan. Amnon would tell his dad he was ill. He would ask David to send Tamar to nurse him and bring him some *"special bread (made) in my sight so I may eat it from her hand"* (2 Samuel 13:6). King David, a man with an EQ not as high as his IQ, sent word to Tamar to put on her apron and trot over to Amnon's room to make therapeutic pancakes.

The rape transcript shows Tamar trying desperately to fend off Amnon, who did not understand the meaning of NO! She even alluded to the fact that the king might give her to him in marriage. Evidently the laws prohibiting marriage between a half-brother and a half-sister were not yet on the books. But Amnon did not have matrimony in mind.

Even worse, when daylight came and the wild oats needed harvesting Amnon pulled a Dr. Jekyll and Mr. Hyde. According to 2 Samuel 13:15, *"Then Amnon hated her with intense hatred. In fact, he hated her more than he had loved her."*

Tamar appealed to his nonexistent sense of honor by telling him, *"Sending me away would be a greater wrong than what you have already done to me"* (2 Samuel 13:16). Nevertheless, Amnon turned to his body servant and instructed him to, *"Get this woman out of here"* (2 Samuel 13:17). Tamar ran sobbing down the palace hall to be stopped by her brother Absalom, who heard her tale and offered her safety in his apartments. Then Absalom waited for a good moment to kill Amnon.

Love Lesson 13   As a young woman, Tamar's tale reminded me of "Little Red Riding Hood." In both stories someone was in bed and someone approached the bedside and was devoured. This cautionary aspect kept me away from strange bedsides for some time. Rhonda Kelley, author of Lessons from Women in the Bible, has another point to make. She focuses on Absalom's vengeance. She notes that "Forgiveness comes from God and restores broken fellowship with Him. God's forgiveness is complete, everlasting, and available to

Unfortunately, the grudge route doesn't lead to a place of healing.

all. Part of the healing process for wounded women today is to forgive the ones who hurt them. Christians are to acknowledge their hurt, freely forgive the offense, and confess any bitterness."

Melody, a volunteer at a rape crisis center, agrees with Kelley's wisdom. She stresses that only God can provide the grace that allows a victim to possess the forgiveness factor. "Too often our society equates forgiveness with wimpdom," says Melody. "Look at the popularity of movies like 'Terminator.' Unfortunately, the grudge route doesn't lead to a place of healing."

Tamar & Amnon in Scripture

2 Samuel 13:6-19

⁶So Amnon lay down and pretended to be ill. When the king came to see him, Amnon said to him, "I would like my sister Tamar to come and make some special bread in my sight, so I may eat from her hand."

⁷David sent word to Tamar at the palace: "Go to the house of your brother Amnon and prepare some food for him." ⁸So Tamar went to the house of her brother Amnon, who was lying down. She took some dough, kneaded it, made the bread in his sight and baked it. ⁹Then she took the pan and served him the bread, but he refused to eat.

"Send everyone out of here," Amnon said. So everyone left him. ¹⁰Then Amnon said to Tamar, "Bring the food here into my bedroom so I may eat from your hand." And Tamar took the bread she had prepared and brought it to her brother Amnon in his bedroom. ¹¹But when she took it to him to eat, he grabbed her and said, "Come to bed with me, my sister."

¹²"Don't, my brother!" she said to him. "Don't force me. Such a thing should not be done in Israel! Don't do this wicked thing. ¹³What about me? Where could I get rid of my disgrace? And what about you? You would be like one of the wicked fools in Israel. Please speak to the king; he will not keep me from being married to you." ¹⁴But he refused to listen to her, and since he was stronger than she, he raped her.

¹⁵Then Amnon hated her with intense hatred. In fact, he hated her more than he had loved her. Amnon said to her, "Get up and get out!"

¹⁶"No!" she said to him. "Sending me away would be a greater wrong than what you have already done to me."

But he refused to listen to her. ¹⁷He called his personal servant and said, "Get this woman out of here and bolt the door after her." ¹⁸So his servant put her out and bolted the door after her. She was wearing a richly ornamented robe, for this was the kind of garment the virgin daughters of the king wore. ¹⁹Tamar put ashes on her head and tore the ornamented robe she was wearing. She put her hand on her head and went away, weeping aloud as she went.

Love Stories From the Bible

Ahab & Jezebel

AHAB & JEZEBEL:
ALL WE DO SHOULD REFLECT GOD'S LOVE.

AHAB & JEZEBEL

As Mr. and Mrs. Rhett Butler demonstrated, some relationships are not good ones. And yet they are useful for instruction. Several biblical couples provide excellent examples of what not to do. Jezebel and Ahab are number one on the Gifts of the Negative Hit Parade. Indeed, during my Deep South childhood, the worst thing one could say about another woman was that she was a "Real Jezebel." That usually meant a big hair woman who was domineering, scheming and promiscuous. Although at one time a newcomer to Jonesboro was dubbed a Jezebel because she hung her undies on the clothesline without pinning them INSIDE pillowcases, as was the small town tradition.

Jezebel is known for her support of the idolatrous cult of Baal. She is also known for her extermination of the prophets (1 King 18:4) and particularly for her persecution of Elijah. She is less well known for her complete obsession with Ahab's kingly persona. Evidently, she considered any disrespect for Ahab to be an attack upon herself. Hence the plot involving the vineyard in 1 Kings 21: 1-14. She had a vineyard owner framed and killed because he refused Ahab's offer of purchase, and she couldn't stand to see Ahab pouting. Devoted, but way overboard.

Love Lesson 14   Literature and history are full of women who walk in Jezebel's stilettos. Lady Macbeth is very invested in being the wife of a powerful man in Shakespeare's tale of intrigue and multiple murders. According to Edith Deen, author of several biblical classics, "in her (Jezebel's) fanaticism, she might be likened to Mary, Queen of Scots. Her death suggests the death of Marie Antoinette. And like Catherine de' Medici, Jezebel is remembered as an outstanding example of what godly women ought not to be." Or to paraphrase a country song lyric, "A woman oughta stand by her man, not stomp on him."

A woman oughta stand by her man, not stomp on him.

Ahab & Jezebel in Scripture

1 Kings 21:1-16

¹Some time later there was an incident involving a vineyard belonging to Naboth the Jezreelite. The vineyard was in Jezreel, close to the palace of Ahab king of Samaria. ²Ahab said to Naboth, "Let me have your vineyard to use for a vegetable garden, since it is close to my palace. In exchange I will give you a better vineyard or, if you prefer, I will pay you whatever it is worth."

³But Naboth replied, "The LORD forbid that I should give you the inheritance of my fathers."

⁴So Ahab went home, sullen and angry because Naboth the Jezreelite had said, "I will not give you the inheritance of my fathers." He lay on his bed sulking and refused to eat.

⁵His wife Jezebel came in and asked him, "Why are you so sullen? Why won't you eat?"

⁶He answered her, "Because I said to Naboth the Jezreelite, 'Sell me your vineyard; or if you prefer, I will give you another vineyard in its place.' But he said, 'I will not give you my vineyard.'"

⁷Jezebel his wife said, "Is this how you act as king over Israel? Get up and eat! Cheer up. I'll get you the vineyard of Naboth the Jezreelite."

⁸So she wrote letters in Ahab's name, placed his seal on them, and sent them to the elders and nobles who lived in Naboth's city with him. ⁹In those letters she wrote:

"Proclaim a day of fasting and seat Naboth in a prominent place among the people. ¹⁰But seat two scoundrels opposite him and have them testify that he has cursed both God and the king. Then take him out and stone him to death."

¹¹So the elders and nobles who lived in Naboth's city did as Jezebel directed in the letters she had written to them. ¹²They proclaimed a fast and seated Naboth in a prominent place among the people. ¹³Then two scoundrels came and sat opposite him and brought charges against Naboth before the people, saying, "Naboth has cursed both God and the king." So they took him outside the city and stoned him to death. ¹⁴Then they sent word to Jezebel: "Naboth has been stoned and is dead."

¹⁵As soon as Jezebel heard that Naboth had been stoned to death, she said to Ahab, "Get up and take possession of the vineyard of Naboth the Jezreelite that he refused to sell you. He is no longer alive, but dead." ¹⁶When Ahab heard that Naboth was dead, he got up and went down to take possession of Naboth's vineyard.

Love Stories From the Bible

King Ahasuerus & Esther

KING AHASUERUS & ESTHER:
GOD WILL GRANT COURAGE TO
THOSE WHO ASK.

KING AHASUERUS & ESTHER

Esther was a *rara avis*, one of those individuals who was equally gorgeous inside and outside. It was her outside that captured King Ahasuerus, the Alpha male of the era. As the ruler of Persia from 486-465 BC, King Ahasuerus was a "my way or the highway" monarch. When Vasti, his previous queen, had failed to honor a kingly request to party into the wee hours, Ahasuerus had banished her and begun interviewing nubile candidates to fill the queenly vacancy.

In a precursor to reality TV, Esther was one of the many virgins who wanted to marry a king. The king, a man of action, took one look at the sweet faced girl, liked what he saw, and made her the first lady of the land.

The King did not know that she was a Jew. Mordecai, Esther's relative, was a big advocate of *don't ask; don't tell*. The king didn't ask; the queen didn't tell. For a while all was well with the royal couple. Then Haman, an officer in Ahasuerus' court, appeared with his bad haircut and his hatred of Jews. Haman was instrumental in passing a decree that all people must bow or be executed. Jews bowed only to God, so this meant death for Esther and her fellow Jews. Esther faced a dilemma. She could remain quiet about her Jewish heritage and stay the pampered queen, or she could reveal her heritage and risk Ahasuerus' wrath.

Like many a Southern belle who knows bad news goes down better with barbecue, Esther planned a banquet for the king and Haman. After the wine, women and song, she revealed both her Jewish heritage and

Haman's plan to execute her people. Ahasuerus was incensed at Haman. He sentenced Haman to hang on a Jewish gallows. What irony.

Love Lesson 15 Esther is another poster girl for courageous leadership in the feminine mode. Speaking the truth with love is never easy. It is especially difficult when one stands to lose one's love, one's livelihood, or perhaps one's life. Nevertheless, Esther saved her people by speaking out when the times demanded it. A woman who walks in Esther's royal sling back pumps is Dame Cicely Saunders, founder of the modern Hospice movement. In the sixties, she campaigned for the judicious use of drugs to control pain for the terminally ill. It was a radical idea at that time. Now it is an idea that is accepted worldwide.

Many a Southern belle knows bad news goes down better with barbecue.

King Ahasuerus & Esther in Scripture

Esther 5:1-14

[1]On the third day Esther put on her royal robes and stood in the inner court of the palace, in front of the king's hall. The king was sitting on his royal throne in the hall, facing the entrance. [2]When he saw Queen Esther standing in the court, he was pleased with her and held out to her the gold scepter that was in his hand. So Esther approached and touched the tip of the scepter.

[3]Then the king asked, "What is it, Queen Esther? What is your request? Even up to half the kingdom, it will be given you."

[4]"If it pleases the king," replied Esther, "let the king, together with Haman, come today to a banquet I have prepared for him."

[5]"Bring Haman at once," the king said, "so that we may do what Esther asks."

So the king and Haman went to the banquet Esther had prepared. [6]As they were drinking wine, the king again asked Esther, "Now what is your petition? It will be given you. And what is your request? Even up to half the kingdom, it will be granted."

[7]Esther replied, "My petition and my request is this: [8]If the king regards me with favor and if it pleases the king to grant my petition and fulfill my request, let the king and Haman come tomorrow to the banquet I will prepare for them. Then I will answer the king's question."

[9]Haman went out that day happy and in high spirits. But when he saw Mordecai at the king's gate and observed that he neither rose nor showed fear in his presence, he was filled with rage against Mordecai. [10]Nevertheless, Haman restrained himself and went home.

Calling together his friends and Zeresh, his wife, [11]Haman boasted to them about his vast wealth, his many sons, and all the ways the king had honored him and how he had elevated him above the other nobles and officials. [12]"And that's not all," Haman added. "I'm the only person Queen Esther invited to accompany the king to the banquet she gave. And she has invited me along with the king tomorrow. [13]But all this gives me no satisfaction as long as I see that Jew Mordecai sitting at the king's gate."

[14]His wife Zeresh and all his friends said to him, "Have a gallows built, seventy-five feet high, and ask the king in the morning to have Mordecai hanged on it. Then go with the king to the dinner and be happy." This suggestion delighted Haman, and he had the gallows built.

Love Stories From the Bible

Rahab & Salmon

RAHAB & SALMON:
NO ONE IS BEYOND REDEMPTION.

RAHAB & SALMON

Rahab-the-Harlot was always spoken of in hushed tones at Jonesboro Methodist. So, of course, all of us in the hormone zone were fascinated by her tale. It was a classic —bad girl makes good. Rahab- the-Harlot, along with Sarah, became one of the two women mentioned in Hebrews 11 as examples of godly faith. Until I reached the wise and sophisticated age of 15, I thought the pastor was referring to Rahab scornfully as a Protestant— not a prostitute— and I wondered how Protestants could be so bad since as far as I knew, I was one.

It seems Rahab and her family lived in the famous wall of Jericho, in a house that commanded a strategic view of the plains. When Joshua dispatched two spies for an inspection of the formidable wall, Rahab hid them from the king of Jericho in her flax pile; as making linen was her day job.

How did this foreign woman resolve to fear and obey Israel's God? The author of her story does not explain her leap of faith, but the Bible does document her deeds, *"By faith the harlot Rahab did not perish with those who did not believe, when she had received the spies with peace"* (Hebrew 11:31).

In exchange for her effort, Rahab asked that her family be spared in the upcoming invasion. She hung a scarlet thread from her window as a sign to the conquering troops not to harm the inhabitants of the house. After the battle she was received into the nation of Israel. An even more remarkable fact is that she married Salmon, an old money Israelite, and the son to Judah's tribal leader.

Love Lesson 16   From Harlot to Heroine. What a spectacular transformation! Rahab's story told me at 15 —and still tells me— nothing is impossible with the living God. With God one can make amazing changes in all areas of life— physical, mental, or spiritual. Erik Weihenmayer, the first blind climber to summit on Everest, chronicled his incredible transformation from a frightened young man with a visual impairment into a world class climber in his biography, *Touch the Top of the World*. Recounting the thoughts he had upon reaching the summit, he said, "After I had gone blind almost twenty years ago, I would have been proud to find the bathroom, so I said a quick prayer and thanked God for giving me so much." Blind boy to Everest Conqueror, Harlot to Heroine—as the old song goes "Our God is an Awesome God."

Rahab & Salmon in Scripture

Joshua 2:1-21

¹Then Joshua son of Nun secretly sent two spies from Shittim. "Go, look over the land," he said, "especially Jericho." So they went and entered the house of a prostitute named Rahab and stayed there.

²The king of Jericho was told, "Look! Some of the Israelites have come here tonight to spy out the land." ³So the king of Jericho sent this message to Rahab: "Bring out the men who came to you and entered your house, because they have come to spy out the whole land."

⁴But the woman had taken the two men and hidden them. She said, "Yes, the men came to me, but I did not know where they had come from. ⁵At dusk, when it was time to close the city gate, the men left. I don't know which way they went. Go after them quickly. You may **catch up with** them." ⁶But she had taken them up to the roof and hidden them under the stalks of flax she had laid out on the roof. ⁷So the men set out in pursuit of the spies on the road that leads to the fords of the Jordan, and as soon as the pursuers had gone out, the gate was shut.

⁸Before the spies lay down for the night, she went up on the roof ⁹and said to them, "I know that the LORD has given this land to you and that a great fear of you has fallen on us, so that all who live in this country are melting in fear because of you. ¹⁰We have heard how the LORD dried up the water of the Red Sea for you when you came out of Egypt, and what you did to Sihon and Og, the two kings of the Amorites east of the Jordan, whom you completely destroyed. ¹¹When we heard of it, our hearts melted and everyone's courage failed because of you, for the LORD your God is God in heaven above and on the earth below. ¹²Now then, please swear to me by the LORD that you will show kindness to my family, because I have shown kindness to you. Give me a sure sign ¹³that you will

spare the lives of my father and mother, my brothers and sisters, and all who belong to them, and that you will save us from death."

¹⁴"Our lives for your lives!" the men assured her. "If you don't tell what we are doing, we will treat you kindly and faithfully when the LORD gives us the land."

¹⁵So she let them down by a rope through the window, for the house she lived in was part of the city wall. ¹⁶Now she had said to them, "Go to the hills so the pursuers will not find you. Hide yourselves there three days until they return, and then go on your way."

¹⁷The men said to her, "This oath you made us swear will not be binding on us ¹⁸unless, when we enter the land, you have tied this scarlet cord in the window through which you let us down, and unless you have brought your father and mother, your brothers and all your family into your house. ¹⁹If anyone goes outside your house into the street, his blood will be on his own head; we will not be responsible. As for anyone who is in the house with you, his blood will be on our head if a hand is laid on him. ²⁰But if you tell what we are doing, we will be released from the oath you made us swear."

²¹"Agreed," she replied. "Let it be as you say." So she sent them away and they departed. And she tied the scarlet cord in the window.

Love Stories From the Bible

Mary & Joseph

MARY & JOSEPH:
FEAR NOT; THE LORD IS
WITH YOU ALWAYS.

MARY & JOSEPH

Mary and Joseph were what Georgia folks would call a May/December couple. In today's fast-forward world they might have met via personal ad. *Older, settled tradesman seeks younger woman. Objective— start a family.* This might have attracted Mary, a peasant girl. Who might have placed the ad? Joseph of Heli or as the Bible says, *"Joseph son of Jacob,"* a man that some religious traditions have labeled a widower. What a shadowy figure he is, almost disappearing when Jesus reaches adolescence. As a young girl, I felt I knew him. He reminded me of the quiet man with the callused palms who helped restart the family car when the battery failed after one interminable day at church. He was quietly competent, one of those older men who could light the bonfire with a single match and pop a roadside rattler with the rifle he carried in the gun rack of his brown pickup truck.

They must have had quite a conversation the night Mary told him she was pregnant, even though they had not *"known one another,"* which was the biblical term for consummation. Matthew 1:18-21 gives a little insight into Joseph's thoughts. We know his first thought was to *"dismiss her quietly."* This stealth dismissal was important because in Jewish society a public dismissal could have meant Mary's death. The Law said that an adulteress deserved death. Jewish marriages are contracted in two stages, and Joseph and Mary were in between the betrothal and the transferal stages. A word from Joseph, and Mary could have been dragged into the public square and pelted by righteous rock-throwers.

Did Mary think about sharp stones biting into her smooth skin when Joseph left the room, the night she told him about the child? Surely, she knew the law also. When he left to return to his house, he had not promised her a future. In his mind, according to Matthew's gospel, there was no future that included her. The marriage was over. What was the conversation the next morning after the angel had instructed him to proceed with the marriage? Could she have discerned her fate from his face when he entered the room? Was he smiling? Was she relieved? Or was she so confident in God's grace that it never occurred to her to worry?

Love Lesson 17 **Even as an adolescent, I believed Mary had to have some anxiety. True, she was the mother of God, but she was also an unwed mother in a culture that defined a woman as the property of the man she married. She knew that she was on a divine mission, but it must have occurred to her that she didn't know how bumpy the road could be.**

For many of my Deep Dixie friends, the fact that God's redemptive plan required the body of a woman is powerful. It is powerful, too, that the woman had to accede to the plan. She was not merely taken over like a possum on a night hunt. God was not forced upon Mary. She willingly became the instrument of God's plan. The fact that the woman had to act in the face of her fear is also powerful. The angel

For many of my Deep Dixie friends, the fact that God's redemptive plan required the body of a woman is powerful.

does not show Mary the ancient equivalent of a Toys R' Us infomercial in which the face of motherhood is painted beatific blush. Instead, the angel utters, *"Fear Not,"* thereby acknowledging the fact that the event is truly terrifying.

Fr. Edward Harrison, Dean of St. John's Cathedral, Jacksonville, Florida, preached a Christmas sermon on the phrase "Fear not." His point was that if something is not terrifying, it is not an angel. Since "angel" comes from the Greek word Angelos, which translates into "messenger," many terrifying events can be seen as spiritual messengers.

That idea has helped me to see divorce, serious illness, and other life challenges as dark angels. Each teeth-chattering event has helped me learn new skills, develop empathy and understand that life really is what happens while we are planning otherwise. Each terrifying incident has made me aware that I can not handle life myself; I must rely on God to help me through "the valley of the shadow." The bullet battered yield signs I see at the country road intersections remind me that God needs my receptivity in order to birth His mighty plan.

Mary & Joseph in Scripture
Matthew 1:18-25

[18]This is how the birth of Jesus Christ came about: His mother Mary was pledged to be married to Joseph, but before they came together, she was found to be with child through the Holy Spirit. [19]Because Joseph her husband was a righteous man and did not want to expose her to public disgrace, he had in mind to divorce her quietly.

[20]But after he had considered this, an angel of the Lord appeared to him in a dream and said, "Joseph son of David, do not be afraid to take Mary home as your wife, because what is conceived in her is from the Holy Spirit. [21]She will give birth to a son, and you are to give him the name Jesus, because he will save his people from their sins."

[22]All this took place to fulfill what the Lord had said through the prophet: [23]"The virgin will be with child and will give birth to a son, and they will call him Immanuel"-which means, "God with us."

[24]When Joseph woke up, he did what the angel of the Lord had commanded him and took Mary home as his wife. [25]But he had no union with her until she gave birth to a son. And he gave him the name Jesus.

Love Stories From the Bible

Pilate & Mrs. P.

PILATE & MRS. P.:
OURS IS NOT TO BE SUCCESSFUL;
OURS IS TO BE FAITHFUL.

PILATE & MRS. P.

Scripture tells the tale. While Pilate was seated on the judge's seat and having a rough day with the trial of Jesus, his wife sent him this message: *"Don't have anything to do with that innocent man, for I have suffered a great deal today in a dream because of him."* Who was this woman who could speak so freely to her husband, the governor? They must have had a relationship of great respect, for it was unusual for men to listen to women concerning decisions of policy. She must also have been a woman who was attuned to her own inner life. She took a dream to heart and acted on its message without hesitation. Finally, she was a woman of courage. Since she had not been in coma or a convent, she knew the tide of public opinion was certainly running against the Jewish Carpenter. Still, she sent the message.

According to Edith Den, author of *All the Women of the Bible*, Pilate's wife lived in splendor far from the dusty streets of the common people. She was probably living in the Herodian Palace in Jerusalem, a luxurious abode with an area large enough to accommodate a hundred guests. Through them (the porticos) she could see flashing fountains and luxuriant gardens in which cooed flocks of milk-white doves.

Perhaps that is the way she first saw Jesus—through the porticos. Or perhaps she only heard about Him from her husband or overheard her body servants buzzing about the Carpenter's many miracles. Whatever the informational avenue, she begged her husband not to put a just man to death. Edith Deen continues with an interesting point, "Her decision had come as a result of her dream, where she had awakened to two convictions, that Jesus was an innocent man and that her husband would be inviting disaster if by reason of his authority, he should take action against Him."

Love Lesson 18   How often have we seen this pattern—Hillary and Bill, Roselyn and Jimmy, Eleanor and Franklin—the intuitive woman seeking to shield the powerful man from pain in the political arena? And Pilate did hear her. He said that he found no fault in Jesus, but he pulled his authority punches and left it up to the crowd to decide between Barabbas and Christ. The crowd's choice is history.

What is the lesson? Perhaps, it is the old one Pastor Frank used to hammer home at Jonesboro Methodist every second Sunday. It was that we must speak the truth in love. Speaking the truth does not mean we will be liked or even heard. As Mother Teresa said, "Ours is not to be successful; ours is to be faithful." Pilate's wife was faithful to her inner vision. She was not successful. How very sad. Jesus, the just man, was slain; Barabbas, the thief, was set free. But Mrs. P had not been silent.

Pilate and Mrs. P. in Scripture

Matthew 27:19-20

19While Pilate was sitting on the judge's seat, his wife sent him this message: "Don't have anything to do with that innocent man, for I have suffered a great deal today in a dream because of him."

20But the chief priests and the elders persuaded the crowd to ask for Barabbas and to have Jesus executed.

Love Stories From the Bible

Elizabeth & Zechariah

ELIZABETH & ZECHARIAH:
TAKE GOD AT HIS WORD.

ELIZABETH & ZECHARIAH

The perfect corporate couple award goes to John the Baptist's parents. From birth Elizabeth was groomed for her role as wife. She was the daughter of a priest and married a priest, Zechariah. The loving couple lived in Judea, an area not far from Jerusalem. He commuted to the Temple while she kept the home fires burning. Unfortunately, she was barren, which in biblical times carried the same sadness as it does today for couples who want children. But, unlike today, there were few alternatives. A childless woman in Elizabeth's day carried a social stigma. Barrenness suggested that God had judged the woman and found her wanting. For a priest's wife, this implication of infertility had to cut to the bone.

Nevertheless, the Bible says that Elizabeth and her husband did not shake their fists at the Almighty. Indeed, they were *righteous before God, walking in all the commandments and ordinances of the Lord blameless* (Luke 1:6). As did Sarah and Abraham, this couple drew strength from their shared belief in God's purpose and plan.

Then the miracle! Although she was aged, Elizabeth conceived. When the angel told her husband about the conception, he questioned the possibility—and he was rendered speechless. According to the Bible, the angel Gabriel told Zechariah that he had shown insufficient faith, and as a result of this failure, he would not speak again until their baby was born. Talk about stress on a marriage! A late in life baby and a husband who can't comment on nursery space, possible names and the urgent desire for the 2:00 a.m. bag of chips.

They must have exchanged nods and notes, however, because when the moment came for the all-important naming, both Elizabeth and Zechariah agreed that their child would be named John. Their friends were puzzled. Some had already begun calling the long awaited son Zechariah, Jr., after his silent dad. A few of the couple's close friends must have assumed that Elizabeth was taking advantage of her husband's disability when she said John was to be the child's name. One can only imagine the release of tension and relief in Elizabeth's soul when Zechariah scrawled the sentence *His name is John* (Luke 1:63). One can only imagine also her delight when her husband's voice boomed once again in prayer and praise at the birth of his son John.

Talk about stress on a marriage!

Love Lesson 19 **Elizabeth's story appeared on my mental screen recently when I watched two young neighbors descend into infertility hell. Life for them became an endless round of estrogen injections, temperature taking, lab reports, and conversations that inevitably circled around to their latest failure. Their focus on conception caused them to doubt the love of God and sometimes their love for one another. Elizabeth and Zechariah prayed for progeny (Luke 1:13), but they also continued to worship God through attending Temple and providing hospitality (Luke 1:40).**

And to their credit, my friends persevered in their faith and in their attempts to conceive. I'm happy to report they were rewarded with a daughter.

Elizabeth & Zechariah in Scripture

Luke 1:5-64

[5]In the time of Herod king of Judea there was a priest named Zechariah, who belonged to the priestly division of Abijah; his wife Elizabeth was also a descendant of Aaron. [6]Both of them were upright in the sight of God, observing all the Lord's commandments and regulations blamelessly. [7]But they had no children, because Elizabeth was barren; and they were both well along in years.

[8]Once when Zechariah's division was on duty and he was serving as priest before God, [9]he was chosen by lot, according to the custom of the priesthood, to go into the temple of the Lord and burn incense. [10]And when the time for the burning of incense came, all the assembled worshipers were praying outside.

[11]Then an angel of the Lord appeared to him, standing at the right side of the altar of incense. [12]When Zechariah saw him, he was startled and was gripped with fear. [13]But the angel said to him: "Do not be afraid, Zechariah; your prayer has been heard. Your wife Elizabeth will bear you a son, and you are to give him the name John. [14]He will be a joy and delight to you, and many will rejoice because of his birth, [15]for he will be great in the sight of the Lord. He is never to take wine or other fermented drink, and he will be filled with the Holy Spirit even from birth.

[16]Many of the people of Israel will he bring back to the Lord their God. [17]And he will go on before the Lord, in the spirit and power of Elijah, to turn the hearts of the fathers to their children and the disobedient to the wisdom of the righteous-to make ready a people prepared for the Lord." [18]Zechariah asked the angel, "How can I be sure of this? I am an old man and my wife is well along in years."

[19]The angel answered, "I am Gabriel. I stand in the presence of God, and I have been sent to speak to you and to tell you this good news. [20]And now you

will be silent and not able to speak until the day this happens, because you did not believe my words, which will come true at their proper time."

²¹Meanwhile, the people were waiting for Zechariah and wondering why he stayed so long in the temple. ²²When he came out, he could not speak to them. They realized he had seen a vision in the temple, for he kept making signs to them but remained unable to speak.

²³When his time of service was completed, he returned home. ²⁴After this his wife Elizabeth became pregnant and for five months remained in seclusion. ²⁵"The Lord has done this for me," she said. "In these days he has shown his favor and taken away my disgrace among the people."

²⁶In the sixth month, God sent the angel Gabriel to Nazareth, a town in Galilee, ²⁷to a virgin pledged to be married to a man named Joseph, a descendant of David. The virgin's name was Mary. ²⁸The angel went to her and said, "Greetings, you who are highly favored! The Lord is with you."

²⁹Mary was greatly troubled at his words and wondered what kind of greeting this might be. ³⁰But the angel said to her, "Do not be afraid, Mary, you have found favor with God. ³¹You will be with child and give birth to a son, and you are to give him the name Jesus. ³²He will be great and will be called the Son of the Most High. The Lord God will give him the throne of his father David, ³³and he will reign over the house of Jacob forever; his kingdom will never end."

³⁴"How will this be," Mary asked the angel, "since I am a virgin?"

³⁵The angel answered, "The Holy Spirit will come upon you, and the power of the Most High will overshadow you. So the holy one to be born will be called the Son of God. ³⁶Even Elizabeth your relative is going to have a child in her old age, and she who was said to be barren is in her sixth month. ³⁷For nothing is impossible with God."

³⁸"I am the Lord's servant," Mary answered. "May it be to me as you have said." Then the angel left her.

³⁹At that time Mary got ready and hurried to a town in the hill country of Judea, ⁴⁰where she entered Zechariah's home and greeted Elizabeth. ⁴¹When Elizabeth heard Mary's greeting, the baby leaped in her womb, and Elizabeth was filled with the Holy Spirit. ⁴²In a loud voice she exclaimed: "Blessed are you among women, and blessed is the child you will bear! ⁴³But why am I so favored, that the mother of my Lord should come to me? ⁴⁴As soon as the sound of your greeting reached my ears, the baby in my womb leaped for joy. ⁴⁵Blessed is she who has believed that what the Lord has said to her will be accomplished!"

⁴⁶And Mary said:

"My soul glorifies the Lord ⁴⁷and my spirit rejoices in God my Savior, ⁴⁸for he has been mindful of the humble state of his servant. From now on all generations will call me blessed, ⁴⁹for the Mighty One has done great things for me- holy is his name. ⁵⁰His mercy extends to those who fear him, from generation to generation. ⁵¹He has performed mighty deeds with his arm; he has scattered those who are proud in their inmost thoughts. ⁵²He has brought down rulers from their thrones but has lifted up the humble. ⁵³He has filled the hungry with good things but has sent the rich away empty. ⁵⁴He has helped his servant Israel, remembering to be merciful ⁵⁵to Abraham and his descendants forever, even as he said to our fathers."

⁵⁶Mary stayed with Elizabeth for about three months and then returned home.

⁵⁷When it was time for Elizabeth to have her baby, she gave birth to a son. ⁵⁸Her neighbors and relatives heard that the Lord had shown her great mercy, and they shared her joy.

⁵⁹On the eighth day they came to circumcise the child, and they were going to name him after his father Zechariah, ⁶⁰but his mother spoke up and said, "No! He is to be called John."

⁶¹They said to her, "There is no one among your relatives who has that name."

⁶²Then they made signs to his father, to find out what he would like to name

the child. [63]He asked for a writing tablet, and to everyone's astonishment he wrote, "His name is John." [64]Immediately his mouth was opened and his tongue was loosed, and he began to speak, praising God.

Love Stories From the Bible

Sapphira & Ananias

SAPPHIRA & ANANIAS:
TELL THE TRUTH.

SAPPHIRA & ANANIAS

Another gift of the negative. Here's a romance that definitely doesn't have the principals living happily ever after. Sapphira and Ananias were two early church folks who became partners in deceit. They sold property, but kept some of the proceeds for themselves. When Peter asked about the amount of the profits, Ananias lied and then fell dead. Not to be outdone, Sapphira prevaricated on prices and she keeled over also.

As a teenager, I didn't get this one. Where was the God of compassion? This story didn't fit my picture of Jesus praying in the Garden of Gethsemane, golden light streaming from His ash blonde curls. At first glance this couple looked good. They were in business together like Miss Polly and Mr. Ed, my girlfriend Martha Carol's parents. They ran Low Temp Steel and were the only couple I knew who worked together. As a newbie in the world of dating, I liked seeing men treat women as folks with brains, not just breasts.

Then one day I heard Reverend Frank, the pastor at Jonesboro Methodist Church, give a short sermon on the biblical twosome's transgressions. "Companionship is wonderful," he said, "But it must be guided by the Holy Spirit and based on God's will, or it can go bad. A couple that commits its energies to evil can end up in a dark spot indeed.

"What this couple did—withhold money—threatened the entire fabric of that community, a community that held all things in common. Also, some Bible scholars say that it was not the amount they kept, but their pretense at generosity in the amount they gave. You don't lie to the Holy Spirit."

Love Lesson 20   That explanation made a little more sense. The double deathblows acquired some perspective. After all, I knew about things that threatened community. The incursion of the new Highway I-75 threatened to choke off Highway 41, the major artery into Jonesboro. Jonesboro couldn't have people diverted. It was small enough already, as witnessed by the fact that my family had been "the NEW people" in the 350-person town for nine years.

I knew something about pretense, too. I was fairly sure it killed real relationship. Some of the same folks who sat beside me in the wooden pews on Sunday mornings and fanned themselves with Mann's Funeral Home fans marched under sheets with the Klan on an occasional, steamy Saturday night. I could always tell by their shoes and their watches because the sheets never covered either. Hurting community and hypocrisy were high crimes in my adolescent mind. At 15, I made a note in my diary to keep any husband I happened to acquire out of the real estate market. I underlined the note with scarlet ink.

Sapphira & Ananias in Scripture
Acts 5:1-10

¹Now a man named Ananias, together with his wife Sapphira, also sold a piece of property. ²With his wife's full knowledge he kept back part of the money for himself, but brought the rest and put it at the apostles' feet.

³Then Peter said, "Ananias, how is it that Satan has so filled your heart that you have lied to the Holy Spirit and have kept for yourself some of the money you received for the land? ⁴Didn't it belong to you before it was sold? And after it was sold, wasn't the money at your disposal? What made you think of doing such a thing? You have not lied to men but to God."

⁵When Ananias heard this, he fell down and died. And great fear seized all who heard what had happened. ⁶Then the young men came forward, wrapped up his body, and carried him out and buried him.

⁷About three hours later his wife came in, not knowing what had happened. ⁸Peter asked her, "Tell me, is this the price you and Ananias got for the land?"

"Yes," she said, "that is the price."

⁹Peter said to her, "How could you agree to test the Spirit of the Lord? Look! The feet of the men who buried your husband are at the door, and they will carry you out also."

¹⁰At that moment she fell down at his feet and died. Then the young men came in and, finding her dead, carried her out and buried her beside her husband.

Love Stories From the Bible

Priscilla & Aquila

PRISCILLA & AQUILA:
COMPETENCE AND COMMITMENT
LEAD OTHERS TO THE LORD.

PRISCILLA & AQUILA

This duo was an entrepreneurial couple that combined their love of Christianity with their business savvy. They had been forced out of Rome by the Emperor Claudius. The Apostle Paul met them in Corinth. How? Perhaps he saw them working in the hot desert sun and struck up a conversation about the importance of a good lapped seam on a tent. After all, they were tent-makers just as he was. Eventually he sailed for Syria, and they accompanied him.

Like modern corporate nomads, Priscilla and Aquila didn't seem to be attached to any geographical place. They had a skill set that was in demand. Tent-makers in the desert were the equivalent of good plumbers in suburbia or competent computer programmers in Silicon Valley. Anyway, these two entrepreneurs modeled a growing understanding of Christian marriage as a relationship that honors both parties. They heard Apollos, a young man who struck them as *"learned with a thorough knowledge of the Scriptures"* (Acts 18: 24), and they invited Apollos to their home to discuss with him a broader baptism. It seems he knew only the baptism of John the Baptist.

Love Lesson 21 **Reading the few verses that chronicle this pair, I am struck by several things. First, that Priscilla must have been a very skilled woman to make it in the testosterone-laden arena of tent-making. Second, I am touched by the fact that this dual career couple took the time to disciple a younger Christian. It is obvious that they** were both heavily invested in the mentoring process. After a tough day in the tent factory, they were still willing to share the three possible gifts Christians can share with one another—time, talent and treasure. They walked their talk.

My brother and sister-in-law remind me of Priscilla and Aquila's competency and compassion. Doug and Janine are both very skilled individuals who work together in their home renovation and general contracting business. The hours are long, the tasks are grueling—wallpaper stripping, sheet rock ripping, meeting with frothing owners, estimating costs, pulling permits, riding herd on subcontractors, checking insurance, etc. And yet, these two individuals are the Go To pair when someone needs real help. An elderly woman in their church was hospitalized, and it was revealed that her home was in acute disrepair. Doug and Janine spearheaded the repair project. Like Priscilla and Aquila, these two Christians used their time and their talent to offer real help to a sister in Christ. Like the tent-making duo, Doug and Janine have a solid relationship that doesn't succumb to stress because they are constantly attuned to God's call in their lives.

After a tough day, they were still willing to share the three possible gifts Christians can share—time, talent and treasure.

Priscilla & Aquila in Scripture

Acts 18:1-3, 18-19

[1]After this, Paul left Athens and went to Corinth. [2]There he met a Jew named Aquila, a native of Pontus, who had recently come from Italy with his wife Priscilla, because Claudius had ordered all the Jews to leave Rome. Paul went to see them, [3]and because he was a tentmaker as they were, he stayed and worked with them.

Acts 18:18-19

[19]Paul stayed on in Corinth for some time. Then he left the brothers and sailed for Syria, accompanied by Priscilla and Aquila. Before he sailed, he had his hair cut off at Cenchrea because of a vow he had taken. [19]They arrived at Ephesus, where Paul left Priscilla and Aquila.

The Final Lesson

My grandmother Mimi used to say that the Bible is God's love letter to His people, and that the love letter is a good read. I like that idea. As the revivalists shouted in the tent meetings of my youth, God is love. I've never doubted that fact.